CONCILIUM

Religion in the Eighties

CONCILIUM

Editorial Directors

General Secretariat: Prins Bernhardstraat 2, 6521 AB Nijmegen, The Netherlands

Concilium 178 (2/1985): Liturgy

CONCILIUM

List of Members

Advisory Committee: Liturgy

BLESSING
AND
POWER

Edited by
Mary Collins
and
David Power

English Language Editor
Marcus Lefébure

T. & T. CLARK LTD
Edinburgh

April 1985
T. & T. Clark Ltd, 36 George Street, Edinburgh EH2 2LQ
ISBN: 0 567 30058 7

ISSN: 0010-5236

Typeset by C. R. Barber & Partners (Highlands) Ltd, Fort William
Printed by Page Brothers (Norwich) Ltd

Concilium: Published February, April, June, August, October, December.
Subscriptions 1985: UK: £19.95 (including postage and packing); USA: US$40.00
(including air mail postage and packing); Canada: Canadian$50.00 (including air mail
postage and packing); other countries: £19.95 (including postage and packing).

CONTENTS

Part III
Special Questions

Editorial

THE EDITORIAL decision to explore the relationship of blessing and power in the 1985 Liturgy issue of *Concilium* was prompted by the expectation that the *Rituale Romanum. . .de Benedictionibus*, the official book of blessings, was to be promulgated at the end of 1984. This latest of liturgical books comes more than two decades after the 1963 Constitution on the Sacred Liturgy had mandated its preparation as part of the commitment to reform both sacraments and sacramentals.

Blessing is certainly a suitable, if not self-evidently urgent, topic for liturgical researchers. But why link blessing and power? Finally, the explanation must be theological. As religious behaviour, blessing implies some conception of a relationship between divine power and human activity. Christians believe the full power of blessing is that power made known in Jesus who is the Wisdom and Power of God. Yet along the way to understanding ecclesial blessing, investigators must also look at the socio-cultural, psychological, and political contexts of blessing. Blessing occurs in power-laden situations. Blessing is common human behaviour, a religious transaction of non-Christians as well as Christians that employs word and gesture to disclose and effect salutary relationships. (Its opposite, malediction or curse to effect a destructive relationship, is equally familiar.) Precisely as intelligible human behaviour blessing is also a medium of the divine disclosure that God intends a beneficial relationship with the world in Christ.

Biblical literature and religion offer an obvious starting point for the study of blessing in the Christian tradition. The Old and New Testaments provide ample data for understanding blessing as both grateful praise of God and revelation of God's beneficence. Scripture documents the phenomenon of the institutionalisation of blessing. It also witnesses to the tendency to yoke efficacious blessing to official deeds of those men whose office or status authorises them to act in God's Name and on God's behalf or in the people's name and on their behalf.

Rich and complex as it is, the biblical tradition does not exhaust the resources available for the study of the forms and meaning of blessing within the Christian tradition. The rabbinic tradition had its impact. Further, various cultural milieux past and present in which the Church has taken shape have contributed both to the forms of blessing and to the interpretation of the experienced presence of God in the event of blessing. Conceptions of God, perceptions of the significance of worship, understandings of sin, assumptions about the created world, and actual social structures operative in any given culture and epoch inevitably have impact on expectations of the availability of divine power in the act of blessing or in the related acts of cursing and exorcism.

The late twentieth century is undoubtedly the most complex epoch yet in the history of ecclesial blessing. A high tradition of institutionalised blessing is incorporated into the reformed rites of Vatican II, in the blessings of the Roman Sacramentary, the Pontifical, and the forthcoming Book of Blessings. The official rites of these books are supplemented by local and regional collections of official blessings. But all of this is complemented and interpreted by actual ecclesial praxis. What is actually going on in the life of the Church? In some places, tacit suppression of ecclesial blessing reflects a good measure of ambivalence about its place in a community of believers. In other locales, appreciation of religious blessing persists or it is coming into new prominence in new forms among believers.

The phenomenon of effective blessing in the name of Jesus is neither limited to nor unrelated to the ecclesiastical institutionalisation of the power of Jesus. Certainly, human mediation is part of the structure of all blessing once we get beyond the Genesis narrative of God's direct blessing of creation. Yet the mediation of blessing is expressed in forms much more varied than those blessings reserved for ordained ministers of the Church.

There is considerable ambiguity in the lived experience of believers on which the theological community must reflect as it considers the relationship between human deeds of blessing and the saving power revealed in Jesus. In the weeks the editors were preparing the issue, I had occasion to spend a Sunday in an Indian village high in the ruggedly beautiful but humanly inhospitable mountains that dominate the state of Guererro in Mexico. Our party visited at the thatched hut which was the home of Josefina and her family, and then she joined us as we climbed higher yet to reach the small hut of her 95-year-old grandmother.

We were surprised when our social visit became the occasion for the younger woman's bitter accusation that her grandmother had treated her poorly over the years. To break the tension of the moment our host introduced the business which had brought us up the mountainside. He had a white burial cloth for the elderly woman, something she had requested on an earlier visit, so that she would be ready for death when it came. The cloth, an ordinary white sheet, was embroidered with the cross and an epigram linking her baptism as an infant to her long-awaited death.

When family and neighbours gathered from nearby huts to view the cloth, Josefina again seized the initiative. She knelt in front of her grandmother and presented her with a votive candle and a small bouquet of the golden flowers characteristically presented for the dead. Then she asked for a blessing. The grandmother, who only minutes before had denied the younger woman's accusation, repeated in this dramatic setting her solemn word that she always had and always would intend her only good. Then both women embraced before the onlookers and wept profusely.

Our host and long-time friend of the two women suggested later that Josefina, not unlike some composite of the biblical Jacob and his ingenious mother Rebekah, had indeed manipulated the situation and stolen a blessing in order to assure her own future in the village after the revered elder's death. Various quarrels over many months (including conflict about visits from outsiders like ourselves) had resulted in her being marginalised, even ostracised by other villagers. She needed reconciliation and reintegration to live at peace with her community. Her grandmother, an elder who also received strangers, apparently had the power to bless her and so to improve the deteriorating situation. Josefina took a chance on that power to save. To give herself a future, she asked for and got a public blessing.

The blessing was humanly effective. Reconciliation, hope and promise were palpable. Was it Christian blessing? Was it an ecclesial act? Was what was accomplished done by the power of the Holy Spirit of Jesus? What relationship is there between such spontaneous acts of reconciliation and the Church's hierarchically mediated sacramental reconciliation, whether in the Eucharist or the sacrament of penance? What is the connection between any such humanly intelligible behaviour and the formal and official blessings of the new Roman book? These are theological questions, and the reader's starting points—the worldview operative at the outset of theological reflection—necessarily influence theological judgments about each realm of blessing, that embodied in the Roman book of blessings and that lived in the world of Josefina and her grandmother, what the scholars call the realm of popular religiosity.

This *Concilium* investigation of the foundations, the forms, and the practice of blessing as a manifestation of power has *three parts*. A first section on the tradition of blessing looks at *biblical foundations* and at a subsequent development within the tradition regarding the Church's blessing of things. Irene Nowell investigates the Book of Genesis, where the foundation is laid for understanding the radical structure of the divine-human relationship of blessing which contains within itself an ethical imperative: those whom God blesses are empowered and sent to be a blessing. Next, Rinaldo Fabris considers the biblical notion of the efficacious word as a foundation for understanding words of power—blessings, curses, and exorcisms—in the ministry of Jesus and that of his earliest disciples. Then David Power provides an overview of the Church's long-standing practice of blessing things. He identifies latent tensions and ambiguities which must be taken into account in any contemporary interpretation or reinterpretation of that practice.

The second set of essays in the collection focuses on a particular ecclesial act, the blessing of *baptismal waters*. Our authors were asked to identify ways in which both theological and cultural worldviews enter into and modify what might at first glance seem to be a unitary, coherent, and self-evident Christian activity. But what the realm of water signifies in any culture, what meaning it has within the created world, influences how the local church takes up its relationship with water as suitable mediator of the mystery of Christ. Gabriele Winkler and Alex Stock show that the early Christian East and West with their distinct religious cultures generated distinctive liturgical rites of blessing. Laurent Mpongo presents contemporary black Africa as another cultural reality. It, too, has its own sensibilites about the cosmic power of water. That cultural outlook will inevitably influence the black African people's understanding of water's role in the baptismal mediation of their relationship to God in the Holy Spirit of Jesus. It will influence their appreciation of how water must be blessed.

Pastoral and theological studies constitute the third part of this collection. Janet Walton reports on the contemporary Christian feminist commitment to a mutual rather than a hierarchical understanding of blessing in the Christian community, since the latter consistently and inevitably diminishes women humanly and spiritually. Theologically, Christian feminism locates the power for the ecclesial act of blessing in the power of Baptism with its gift of the indwelling Spirit. Walton's discussion constitutes a critique of the conventional ecclesiastical perspective which makes ordination the source of power for effective ecclesial blessing. In the interview which she gave to Jacques Pohier, Françoise Dolto gives us a psychiatrist's view of the interaction between persons set up by acts of blessing and cursing.

Josep Lligadas, working with a draft and not the final *editio typica* of the Roman volume *De Benedictionibus*, reviews it and then asks some critical questions about the socio-cultural and theological foundations of this most recent product of the liturgical renewal. Finally, J. M. R. Tillard, reflecting from within the living tradition of ecclesial blessing, with all its authentic and inauthentic moments of disclosure of power, provides a systematic theological treatment of *epiclesis*. He identifies epiclesis as the heart of all Christian liturgical prayer and so the touchstone for an evangelically sound understanding of sacramentality and of that form of prayer which is blessing.

As David Power's editorial conclusion underscores, the topic of blessing and power is only introduced in this volume, not exhausted. The editors hope that what is begun here will stimulate readers to further reflection on and investigation of this important aspect of Christian life. The full tradition of ecclesial blessing ought neither to be uncritically dismissed nor uncritically embraced.

MARY COLLINS

PART I

Foundational Articles

Irene Nowell

The Narrative Context of Blessing in the Old Testament

'I HAVE set before you life and death, the blessing and the curse. Choose life . . .' (Deut. 30:19). The parallelism in this exhortation from Deuteronomy indicates that blessing is equivalent to life, curse equivalent to death. The texts which describe blessing support the integral relationship between blessing and life. In the biblical context blessing is the sharing in the life of God which begins with creation and the power to pass on that life by virtue of the blessing of creation. This sharing in the life of God and power to pass on that life continues in the covenant and extends also to sharing of life among God's covenant people. The responsibility imposed by blessing, this sharing of life, is the responsibility to affirm and nurture all life and to contribute by one's own life to the life of the world.[1]

The texts to be examined include texts in which God blesses directly and texts in which human beings call down God's blessing. The texts can be divided into those concerning creation blessing and those concerning covenant blessing. The texts will be examined according to structure, content, and the surrounding context. Conclusions will be drawn concerning the nature of blessing and the implications of biblical blessing in our own day.

1. STRUCTURE, CONTENT, AND CONTEXT OF BLESSING IN THE OT

(a) Creation Blessings: Blessings by God

The form and content of biblical blessing are firmly established by the creation blessings in Genesis 1. Twice in that chapter God blesses the creatures

3

he has made (Gen. 1:22, 28). The two blessings have a similar pattern. There is an introductory phrase announcing: 'God blessed them, saying . . . .' This is followed by God's words, a series of imperatives. In Gen. 1:22 the sea creatures and birds are blessed:

'Be fruitful (imperative of *prh*);
be many (imperative of *rbh*);
fill (imperative of *ml'*) the waters of the sea;
and let the birds be many (jussive of *rbh*) over the earth' (Gen. 1:22).

In Gen. 1:28 the introduction to the blessing of human beings (*hā'ādām*) is more formal: 'God blessed them and God said to them.' The first three imperatives are the same as those in 1:22, but two more imperatives are added:

'Be fruitful (imperative of *prh*);
be many (imperative of *rbh*);
fill (imperative of *ml'*) the earth;
subdue it (imperative of *kbš*);
have dominion over (imperative of *rdh*) the fish of the sea, the birds of the sky, and all living things that creep on the earth' (Gen. 1:28).

The two blessings include within the creative act itself the power to participate in creation, to share the life given by God in creation. They include fertility, the power to increase in number, and to fill the space proper to them.[2] The two additional imperatives in 1:28 give human beings power and responsibility, specifically over the other creatures who were blessed in 1:22.[3]

Several key words emerge within these blessings and in the immediate context. Three verbs are repeated in both blessings: 'Be fruitful' (*prh*), 'be many' (*rbh*), 'fill' (*ml'*). Two additional verbs complete the blessing in 1:28: 'subdue' (*kbš*) and 'have dominion' (*rdh*). Within the immediate context of the two blessings the word 'create' (*br'*), used only for God's creative activity, occurs four times, once in 1:21 and three times in 1:27 introducing the more formal blessing of 1:28. The word *'ādām*, 'human creature', also occurs twice (1:26, 27).

A further blessing occurs at the end of the Priestly account of creation (Gen. 2:3–4). The blessing is in a different form. It is simply reported without direct citation of the words of blessing. It contributes, however, three points to the notion of creation blessing. First of all, the key word *bārā'*, 'create', is found twice more (2:3, 4) and an additional word, *tôlĕdôth*, 'generation', 'genealogy' (from the root *yld*, 'to beget', 'to give birth') is added to the cluster. Secondly, the link between blessing and holiness is established. The content of blessing for the seventh day is another expression of sharing life and creative power with God, i.e., holiness: 'God blessed the seventh day and [thus] made it holy'. Finally, blessing is made an integral part of the climax of the Priestly creation account. The story of creation is told as an explanation of the holiness of the sabbath. The sabbath is holy because of the blessing of God, because of its share in God's creative activity and its return of life to God, refreshing him after his work. Blessing is thus firmly linked to creation and life.

There are two other blessings in the primeval history (Genesis 1–11). Each of them confirms and elucidates the basic pattern established in Genesis 1. Genesis 5 is the Priestly link between Adam and Noah. It is the second genealogy, the second *tôlĕdôth*, of the primeval history (the first being the *tôlĕdôth* of the heavens and the earth, Gen. 2:4). Just as blessing was a significant part of the first *tôlĕdôth*, so it is part of the second (5:2). The key words *bārā'*, 'create', and *'ādām*, 'human creature', 'Adam', are each repeated three times in 5:1–2. The position of this report of blessing between the statement of creation (5:1) and the genealogy of Adam's descendants indicates the connection between the life given at creation and fertility, the power to share life, to share in God's creative act. This is further indicated by the repeated statement that God made *'ādām* 'male and female' (see Gen. 1:27). Human sexuality is part of the blessing of creation. The life and the power to pass it on is a sharing in the life and lifegiving power of God: 'When God created *'ādām* he made him in the image and likeness of God; he created them male and female (5:1). A further concept is added to the cluster of concepts surrounding blessing: To be blessed is to be named, to be given not only life but identity. 'When they were created he blessed them and named them *'ādām*' (5:2). The genealogy which follows this report of blessing indicates life in two respects: long life for all who share the blessing and also continuous descendants. The root *yld*, 'to beget', 'to give birth', which is found in *tôlĕdôth*, 'genealogy', is repeated twice in the account of each descendant.[4]

Noah, who ends the genealogy in Genesis 5, is the recipient of the final blessing in the primeval history (Gen. 9:1–7). The blessing of Noah returns to the pattern of the blessings of Genesis 1. It begins with the introduction, 'God blessed Noah and his sons and said to them'. The blessing itself begins with the three imperatives of Genesis 1: 'be fruitful' (*prh*); 'be many' (*rbh*); 'fill the earth' (*ml'*). The blessing closes (9:7) with a similar list of imperatives: 'be fruitful' (*prh*); 'be many' (*rbh*); 'abound' ('swarm'!, *šrs*); 'be many' (*rbh*).[5]

Between these two series of imperatives is an instruction on responsibility for life. The living creatures over which human beings have dominion will live in fear of them (9:2). Human dominion extends from power to nurture life as far as power to destroy life. This power over life, however, must be used responsibly. Living creatures may be killed for food, in order to sustain human life (9:3); but humans may never forget that life belongs to God. Blood, the symbol of life, belongs to God and may not be eaten (see Lev. 17:11–12, 14; Deut. 12:23–24). Above all, human life is to be protected and human bloodshed avoided, 'for in the image of God has *'ādām* been made' (Gen. 9:6).[6]

The blessing of Noah ends the creation blessings. It forms an inclusion with them by the repetition of the three (or four) major imperatives. It draws out the further implication that life belongs to God. Power over life is shared with human beings through the blessing which is part of their creation. This power includes the power of fertility, increase, and dominion. This power, however, also calls human beings to responsibility for life and respect for the power of God which gives and sustains life.

The blessing of Noah leads from creation blessing to covenant blessing. Immediately following the blessing of Noah, God establishes a covenant with Noah and his descendants, and also with all the living creatures (9:8–10). God's covenant is a promise of life for all living creatures on the earth (Gen. 9:11–17).

(b) Covenant Blessings

(i) Blessings by God

The covenant blessing which is the paradigm for all further covenant blessings is the blessing of Abraham. Three blessings of Abraham must be considered (Gen. 12:1–3; 17:15–19; 22:15–18). The first blessing (Gen. 12:1–3) begins the narrative of the history of God's people just as the blessings of Genesis 1 begin the narrative of creation. This first blessing is primarily God's declaration of blessing.[7] Several concepts which are related to creation blessing can be distinguished. The blessing will result in increase: 'I will make you a great nation'. The blessing gives Abraham a name and an identity: 'I will make your name great' (see 11:41). The blessing implies responsibility: It is in Abraham that all other families of the earth will find blessing,[8] will find their share in this life shared with God.

The blessings of the patriarchs are consistently set in the context of journey. It is in a situation in which life seems to be threatened and familiar life to be lost, that the blessing of God is encountered. Blessing seems to be preceded by the demand to risk the very things which blessing brings—life, family, descendants, land. Blessing, which implies sharing, seems to be preceded by a situation which looks like alienation, like curse, like death. The blessing of Abraham in Genesis 12 is preceded by the demand that Abraham leave land and family (*môladeth*, from the root *yld*, 'to beget', 'to give birth'), and is followed by the simple statement: 'Abram went as the Lord directed him' (12:4).

The blessing of Abraham becomes more specific in Genesis 17. The structure of Gen. 17:16 is similar to that of Gen 12:1–3, three clauses beginning with 'I will', followed by a climactic statement of consequence. God is clearly the originator of blessing. The blessing differs from Gen. 12:3, however, in that it is directed initially to Sarah and then to Isaac.[9] Abraham is informed, first of all, that Sarai will have a new name, Sarah, indicating her identity as sharer in the blessing.[10] Sarah's blessing results in fertility: Sarah will have a son (17:16; see *yld*, 'to give birth', in 17:19, 21). The blessing will be extended to the son. He too will be fruitful and his descendants will have dominion.

The blessing is set within a web of name-giving. At the beginning of Genesis 17, God gives Abram the new name, Abraham, as he establishes the covenant with him (17:5). Sarai's name is changed in the context of the blessing. Abraham's response to God's word of blessing is laughter: 'Abraham fell on his face and laughed' (*yiṣḥāq*, Gen. 17:17). The name of the child to be born is 'he will laugh', Isaac (*yiṣḥāq*, Gen. 17:19; cf. 18:12–15; 21:5–7). The name-giving is associated in each case with covenant making, the establishment of a relationship which gives identity (17:4–5, 16, 19, 21).

The third blessing addressed to Abraham follows the ultimate demand made by God to risk the sign of the blessing: 'Take your son Isaac, your only one, whom you love, and . . . offer him up as a holocaust' (Gen. 22:2). After Abraham takes the risk (and is spared the sacrifice) the Lord declares his blessing (Gen. 22:16–18). The blessing is enclosed by a clause giving Abraham's faith as reason for the blessing. Because Abraham was willing to surrender the blessing—the life and the promise—to God, therefore Abraham is guaranteed the blessing. The Lord swears by himself (22:15) to bless him. The blessing itself repeats the promise of Genesis 12 and echoes the content of the creation blessing of Genesis 1: blessing, fertility, and dominion. The rhetoric is heightened, however, in this blessing promised under oath: 'Blessing I will bless you; multiplying I will multiply your seed.'[11] The blessing ends with the closing formula of Gen. 12:3, extended now to Abraham's descendants: In them all the nations of the earth will find blessing.

God reaffirms the continuation of the blessing through Isaac in Genesis 26. The situation is again one of alienation and sojourning. Isaac is travelling because of the famine in the land. Yahweh appears to him, telling him to sojourn in the land as he directs (26:2, see Gen. 12:1). Yahweh then speaks a blessing which is in continuity with the blessing of Abraham: 'I will be with you and bless you; for to you and your descendants I will give all these lands, in fulfilment of the oath that I swore to your father Abraham' (26:3). The blessing reaffirms the promise of numerous descendants and the pledge that in them all the nations of the earth shall find blessing. The blessing closes with the reminder that it is because of Abraham's obedience that all these blessings come. A later blessing in the same chapter (26:24) repeats the promise of blessing and descendants for the sake of Abraham. A new emphasis in the blessings of Isaac is the promise of presence: 'You have no need to fear, since I am with you' (26:24; see. 26:3).

There are three blessings in which God speaks directly to Jacob, Gen. 28:13–15, 32:29; 35:9–12. In the first (Gen. 28:13–15), Jacob is sojourning, on his way to Haran to find a wife. At Bethel Yahweh appears to him in sleep and says: 'I, Yahweh, am the God of your forefather Abraham and the God of Isaac' (28:13). The link is thus formed with the former bearers of covenant blessing. The content of the blessing reiterates the promise of Yahweh's presence, of land, and of many descendants in whom the nations will find blessing. Yahweh promises protection to Jacob and fidelity to the promise (28:15).

The second blessing occurs also in the context of sojourning. Jacob is on his way to meet Esau when he meets a stranger at the ford of the Jabbok. The stranger wrestles with Jacob until daybreak, at which point he pleads to be released. Jacob, however, will not let him go unless the stranger blesses him. The blessing is the gift of a name, Israel, 'one who has wrestled with God' (32:29).

The third blessing (Gen. 35:9–12) summarises the content of patriarchal blessing. Jacob arrives back at Bethel and God appears to him again and blesses him. His new name is confirmed (35:10). He is commanded to be fruitful (*prh*) and to be many (*rbh*, Gen. 35:11; cf. Gen. 1:28). His descendants are assured of dominion and possession of the land (35:12).

(ii) Blessings by Human Beings

With the passing on of the blessing to Jacob, Isaac's son, two kinds of blessing intersect. God blesses Jacob directly as he blessed Abraham and Isaac; Isaac himself, however, also calls down the blessing of God on his son, the future bearer of the covenant.

Isaac blesses his son twice, the first time unwittingly (Gen. 27:27–29). The content of the blessing is expected: fertility, specifically of the earth, and dominion, even over his brothers. The blessing ends with an allusion to the blessing of Abraham, that those who curse the one who is blessed will in turn be cursed, those who bless him will be blessed.

The unexpected points in this blessing are three: the one giving the blessing, the one receiving the blessing, and the effectiveness of the blessing itself. The transmission of the blessing from creation to Adam, from Adam to Abraham, and from Abraham to Isaac was effected directly by God. In the blessing of

Jacob by his father Isaac, a human being claims the power to transmit the blessing, the sharing in God's life and power.[12] The initial irony of the situation comes in the transmission of the blessing to an unintended recipient. God will bless whom he will bless, regardless of human intentions (see Exod. 34:19). Isaac intends to bless his elder son Esau. Jacob, however, through his mother's plotting, prepares himself and receives the blessing instead. Although human agents have the power to call down the blessing of God, the control of the blessing remains with God. The further irony is that the unintended blessing is effective. Despite Isaac's intentions he has in fact blessed Jacob and he cannot take it back (Gen. 27:37–38). The power of the word, effective in creation, remains effective in the sharing of creation life which is blessing. The blessing has created Jacob, given him life and identity, and it cannot be retracted.[13]

A primary agent in Jacob's acquiring of the covenant blessing is his mother, Rebecca (see 27:5–17). She, like Sarah, was also the recipient of a blessing (Gen. 24:60). As she leaves her family to become Isaac's bride, they call down upon her the blessings of fertility for herself and dominion for her descendants. She is the human agent who actively decides that Jacob will receive the covenant blessing instead of Esau. Therefore Jacob receives the covenant blessing from both his mother and his father.

The second time Isaac blesses Jacob he knows who the recipient is (28:1–4). He sends his son, again a sojourner, to find a wife from his own kindred, and calls down upon him ancient blessing of fruitfulness (*prh*) and increase (*rbh*), the ancient blessing of Abraham, of creation.

From Jacob the blessing is extended to the whole people (Gen. 49:1–28). The content of Jacob's farewell discourse to his sons is primarily a declaration of tribal destinies. His blessing of Joseph (49:22–26) is most like earlier blessings in structure and content.[14]

2. THE NATURE OF OLD TESTAMENT BLESSING

The nature of all further Old Testament blessings is established by the pattern set in the creation and covenant blessings. Blessing is essentially a sharing in life and a sharing of the power of life.[15] This fact is illustrated both by the content of the blessings themselves and by the context in which they are situated.

(a) Content

The key words and concepts in the content of Old Testament blessings indicate, first of all, the abundance and overflow of life. Primary among key words are *prh*, 'be fruitful' (Gen. 1:22, 28; 9:1, 7; 28:3; 35:11) and *rbh*, 'be many' (Gen. 1:22, 28; 9:1, 7; 22:17; 26:4, 24; 28:3; 35:11). These verbs characterise blessing from creation through Jacob and onward. Even when these key words are absent, the notion of fertility, of many descendants who will fill the earth to its four corners, persists (see Gen. 17:16; 24:60; 27:28; 28:14).

With the notion of abundance and overflow of life is found the concept of power over life and responsibility for life. Human beings are given dominion over creation (Gen. 1:28; 9:7?; cf. 22:17; 24:60; 27:29; 35:11), but with that dominion comes responsibility for life (Gen. 9:2–6). Dominion includes relationship with other people. Those covenanted to God will be a great nation (see Gen. 12:2; 17:16; 28:3; 35:11). Dominion also includes relationship to the rest of creation. Those covenanted to God are promised land (Gen. 26:3; 28:4, 13; 35:12) and given power over living creatures (Gen. 9:2–3; see Gen. 1:28). The responsibility which comes with this power over life includes responsibility for the preservation of life and respect for God from whom life comes and to whom life belongs (Gen. 9:2–6). The share in and the power over life also bring responsibility for the fullness of life for all people. All nations can expect to find blessing in those whom God has blessed (Gen. 12:3; 22:18; 28:14).

The underlying truth in the notion that blessing is a sharing in and power over life is that blessing is a sharing with God. Life belongs to God (see Gen. 9:5). He created human beings in his image and in creation blessed them with a share in his own abundant life. This share in God's life is given to all human beings (Gen. 1:28; 5:1–2). Therefore this overflow of life binds human beings not only to God but also to each other. The effect of blessing is a sharing of life with God who pledges to be present (Gen. 26:3, 24; 28:15). The effect of blessing is a sharing of life with all people (Gen. 12:3; 22:18; 28:14). The effect of blessing is holiness (cf. Gen. 2:3).

(*b*) Context

The contexts which surround blessing emphasise the sharing of life with God and the sharing of life with the human community. Blessings occur in the context of the two primary manifestations of God's sharing of life: God's creation (see *br'*, 'create', Gen. 1:21, 27; 2:3–4; 5:1–2) and God's covenant making with human beings (e.g., Gen. 9:9 ff.; 17:2–4, 19, 21; 26:4; 28:13–15). It is in creation and covenant that human beings find the relationship which gives them identity and a name (Gen. 5:2; 12:2; 17:5, 17, 19; 32:29; 35:10).

This identity, however, this sharing of life with God, never occurs in isolation. Blessing always implies relationship and bonding with other human beings. It is under the name of *'ādām*, the universal human creature, that human beings are blessed in creation (Gen. 1:26–27; 5:1–2; 9:5–6). Their very blessing implies power to share life with further generations. They are blessed 'male and female' (Gen. 1:27; 5:2) and given power to beget and give birth (see *yld*, Gen. 2:4; 5:1, 3 ff.; 17:19, 21). They are given not only power to share creation life, but power to share covenant life. They are blessed, fathers and mothers (see Gen. 17:16; 24:60), and given power to pass the blessing on to their children (see Gen. 27:4, 27–29; 28:3–4; 49:1–28). God continues to identify himself by means of his share in this human community. I am the God of your ancestors, Abraham, Isaac, Jacob (Gen. 26:24; 28:13; cf. 26:3; 28:4; Exod. 2:24).

3. IMPLICATIONS FOR GOD'S COVENANT COMMUNITY

Blessing places two demands on those who are blessed. The demands flow from the nature of blessing itself. First of all, blessing is a share in the life of God. This sharing, although integral to human creation, is beyond human comprehension. Blessing demands a willingness to believe in blessing. The willingness to believe demands a willingness to leave everything else, to risk anything else, for the sake of this share in the life of God (see Gen. 12:1, 22:1–18; 26:2–5; 32:25–31). Blessing demands a willingness to share life with God. Blessing demands holiness.

The second demand is like the first. Blessing, a share in the life of God, is therefore a sharing of life with all other creatures, all other people. This sharing of life is a sharing of responsibility for life. Sharing in God's life implies a sharing in God's creating of life, God's nurturing of life, God's protection of life. Blessing implies care for the land and what it yields. Blessing implies care for the poor and powerless; it demands feeding the hungry, sheltering the homeless, tending the sick, sharing with the dying. Blessing implies the active exercise of dominion to eradicate evil, the evils of war and oppression and needless human suffering. Blessing implies the giving of life so that all others may find blessing. Blessing demands a willingness to share life with all who live. Blessing demands love.

Blessing demands blessing. We have the power to share life with God. Through his Word which lives within us we have the power to share life with each other, the power to sustain, to nourish, to protect, to enrich the life of the world. Being blessed gives us the power and the responsibility to bless in turn. 'I have set before you life and death, the blessing and the curse, Choose life' (Deut. 30:19). Choose blessing!

Notes

1. J. Pedersen *Israel: Its Life and Culture* (London 1926) 182–212 centres his invaluable study of blessing around the concepts of power and life. See also S. Mowinckel *Psalmenstudien* (Amsterdam 1966) 5.5–13.

2. See C. Westermann *Creation* (Philadelphia 1974); (*Schöpfung*, Stuttgart 1971) p. 46 who says: 'That is the basic meaning of the word *bless*: the power to be fertile.' See G. Von Rad *Genesis* (Philadelphia 1972); *Das erste Buch Mose: Genesis*, ATD 2–4; (Göttingen 1972) 56; and M. Maher *Genesis* (OTM 2; Wilmington 1982) p. 27.

3. See Westermann, the work cited in note 2, pp. 50–51.

4. The root *yld* is found in 5:3, 4, 6, 7, 9, 10, 12, 13, 15, 16, 18, 19, 21, 22, 25, 26, 28, 30, 32.

5. The second occurrence of the imperative of *rbh* in 9:7 is frequently amended to the imperative of *rdh*, 'have dominion', in agreement with Gen. 1:28. See *Biblica Hebraica Stuttgartensia*.

6. In this middle section (9:2–6) the key word *'ādām* occurs five times, twice in 9:5 and three times in 9:6.

7. The root *brk*, 'to bless', is repeated five times in Gen. 12:2–3.

8. The Hebrew form of the verb *brk*, 'to bless', in 12:3, may be understood in a passive sense: 'will be blessed in you.' It is more likely, however, that the sense is reflexive: 'will bless themselves through you.' See J. Scharbert *brk*, *Theol. Dict. Old Test.* (*Theologisches Wörterbuch zum Alten Testament*, Stuttgart 1973) 2.297.

9. In place of the feminine pronouns which are found in the Hebrew text in the second half of 17:16, read masculine pronouns with the Septuagint: 'I will bless *him*'; '*he* will be a nation'; 'kings of peoples shall come from *him*'.

10. The fact that both Sarah and Abraham are blessed, as are both Isaac and Rebecca, suggests the blessing of *'ādām*, male and female, in the creation blessings (see Gen. 1:27–28; 5:2).

11. The Hebrew construction, infinitive absolute plus finite form of the same verb, implies emphasis.

12. Von Rad, (in the work cited in note 2, 276) asserts that 'active giving on man's part' is essential for the effectiveness of patriarchal blessing.

13. Note that the 'blessing' of Esau (27:39–40) is really a curse, constructed in direct opposition to the blessing of Jacob.

14. The blessing of Moses (Deut. 33:1–29) is similar to the blessing of Jacob in style and content and again extends the power and benefit of blessing to all the people. R. Clifford *Deuteronomy* (OTM 4; Wilmington 1982) at p. 177 points out that the narration of the future by the covenant leader is itself the blessing.

15. Scharbert, (in the work cited in note 8, 293–294) points out that blessing always implies solidarity between the one giving the blessing and the one receiving it.

Rinaldo Fabris

Blessings, Curses and Exorcism in the Biblical Tradition

HUMAN SPEECH, even when reduced to its informative and expressive functions, still has the power to call. Speaking not only communicates, establishes a relationship, but also produces and creates a new situation. If modern culture tends to favour the informative function proper to science, it still, particularly in the social communications media, produces linguistic situations in which the expressive and 'performative' function of the world is to the fore.[1] The language of advertising uses not so much the persuasive power of information as the efficacy of the spoken or written word in a particular authoritative or suggestive setting.

This process of verbal communication shows an echo of the phenomenon, far more extensive in the ancient world, in which an autonomous operative force was attributed to the word in particular circumstances. Here the word transcribes that power of life or death, good or evil, that underlies the relationships between men and the things of the world. The first few pages of Genesis provide an important example of this conception of the word; the relationship of the first man to the animals is expressed by his giving them names: Gen. 2:18–20. In the Yahwist account, Adam's giving names to all the animals created by God is not only a proof of 'wisdom', according to the Eastern model of catalogues of names, but a sign of the difference of mankind from the animal world and his 'lordship' over it. In ancient-eastern thought, names expressed the essence of a thing; calling it by name meant bringing it into being.[2]

This is the setting for the concept of the efficacy and power of the word in the biblical tradition, initiated in some aspects of the first covenant and prolonged in the Gospel presentation of Jesus and the history of the early Church, as set down in the texts of the Christian canon.

1. THE POWER AND EFFICACY OF THE WORD IN THE OT

The efficacious word *par excellence* is the word of God. God expresses his power through his words. In effect, his word instantly does and produces what it says and expresses. Typical of this is the account of creation set down in the priestly tradition, in which God's word-orders and the immediate description of their effect alternate: 'God said, "Let there be light". And there was light' (Gen. 1:3; and see 1:9, 11; 14:15, 24; Ps. 33:9. The efficacious word of God calls all things into existence and gives consistency and order to the universe. The Isaiah tradition provides a good example of this operative efficacy of the word of God. At the end of the Book of the Consolation of Israel, the author refers back to the opening images of the 'joyful messenger' who precedes the procession of the liberated, and confirms the promise of the saving action of God in these terms: 'Yes, as the rain and the snow come down from the heavens and do not return without watering the earth, making it yield and giving growth to provide seed for the sower and bread for the eating, so the word that goes from my mouth does not return to me empty, without carrying out my will and succeeding in what it was sent to do' (Isa. 55:10–11).

The prophet, called to be the town-crier of this word of God, shares in its power and operative efficacy. So the words of the true prophet, sent by God, are fulfilled by the salvation or ruin of those to whom they are addressed. This understanding of the dynamic efficacy of the word of God, whose mouthpiece the prophet is, runs through the whole prophetic tradition, from the early 'scribe' prophets to the last prophetic voices of the post-exilic period. The seventh century prophet Jeremiah explains his vision of the branch of the Watchful Tree (Heb. shāqēd) with this oracle: 'Then Yahweh said, "Well seen! I too watch over (Heb. shogēd) my word to see it fulfilled" ' (Jer. 1:12). Two centuries later, the prophet Zechariah, in the Introduction to the collection of his visions, asked, 'Did not my words and my orders, with which I charged my servants the prophets, overtake your ancestors?' (Zech. 1:6). In the same way, the deuteronomic tradition puts forward the fulfilment of what the prophets announce in the name of the Lord as a criterion for distinguishing between true and false prophets (see Deut. 18:22; Jer. 28:9; Ezek. 33:33).

This view of the prophet as one whose words are effective and operative is rooted in a cultural context made up of two influences: the figure of the 'Charismatic' man and the situation of the biblical alliance. The figure of the man who speaks from charismatic impulse with effects in the realm of good or ill has a symbolic representation in the OT in the figure of Balaam, whose story, based on an ancient tradition, is recounted in Numbers 22:2–24:25. Balaam, a wandering prophet as were the *bārû* of Mesopotamian culture, was engaged by Balak, King of Moab, to curse the tribe of Israel who were encroaching and settling on his land.[3] The proposition/invitation he puts to the man of vision is an excellent expression of the concept of the efficacy of the prophetic word: 'Look how this people coming from Egypt has overrun the whole countryside; they have settled at my door. Come, please, and curse this people for me, for they are stronger than I am. We may then be able to defeat them and drive them out of the country. For this I know: the man you bless is blessed, the man you curse is accursed.' (Num. 22:5–6).

Before giving an answer to the king's messengers, Balaam seeks directions from Yahweh. In the night God comes to Balaam and tells him his will with regard to the destiny of Israel. He tells him not to go with the messengers and, 'You are not to curse this people, for they are blessed' (22:12). But Balak does not give up. He sends a second group of messengers, 'chiefs, more numerous and more renowned than the first', promising to load Balaam with honours and to do whatever he says. Balaam once more consults the Lord, who allows him to go with them on condition that he is to do nothing 'except what I tell you' (22:20). After the incident of the donkey becoming involved in the drama, Balaam meets Balak, and makes his position quite clear: 'Here I am at your side. May I make myself clear to you now? The word that God puts into my mouth, this I shall speak' (22:38).

The biblical account then goes on, in a crescendo of dramatic effect, with the four oracles of Balaam, who, looking out over the encampments of the Israelites, proclaims, 'obliged to say what God puts into my mouth', a blessing: a prosperous and glorious future. In despair at this turn of events, Balak begs him: 'Very well! Do not curse them. But at least do not bless them!' (23:25). But Balaam insists, 'Have I not told you: whatever Yahweh says, I must do?'. Finally, Balak flies into a rage with Balaam and sends him packing for listening only to the word of the Lord, in these words: 'I brought you to curse my enemies, and you bless them three times over! Be off with you, and go home. I promised to load you with honours. Yahweh himself has deprived you of them' (24:10–11). This episode, inserted by the biblical compiler in the story of the journey of the people of God from the desert of Kadesh to Moab, illustrates the role of the 'charismatic' man under the influence of the irresistible power of God. This carefully orchestrated scenario emphasises the vain efforts of the King of Moab first to direct and then to contest the power that comes direct from God into the words of the man 'with far-seeing eyes . . . who hears the word of God . . . who knows the knowledge of the Most High' (25:15–16). In the end, the King just has to go away, knowing that Balaam's words are decisive for the dealings between Israel and Moab.

The counterposed alternative expressed in the verbs 'bless/curse' (Heb. *bārak/ārar* or *qābab*) in the history of the people of God finds its living context in the alliance. On the model of ancient Oriental treaty formularies, the alliance between God and his people, freed from Egypt, ends in a double series of blessings and curses. The strength of the covenant resides in the firm conviction of operative efficacy of what the words of alternate blessing and curses express. The book of Deuteronomy, which is inspired by the formulations of the alliance, sets out, through an ideal discourse put into the mouth of Moses on the threshold of the promised land, God's conditions for the Lord their God being the God of Israel and for Israel being his people: that they keep his commandments, which concentrate on the basic principle of the total love of God as only Lord. Blessings and curses are the result of fidelity or infidelity to this condition of the alliance—as chapter 28 makes clear. But the efficacy of the words of blessing and cursing also depends on the conditions in which they are spoken or transmitted through writing. This is confirmed in the scene evoked in the text of Deut. 27:11–13: the twelve tribes of Israel are to be divided into two groups of six, each on one of the two facing mountains of Samaria, those on Mount Gerizim to bless the people, and those on Mount Ebal for the curse. This is to be pronounced by the Levites, in a form that mixes the commandments of the alliance with the cursing formula, 'A curse on him who . . .', repeated twelve times, to which all the people reply 'Amen' (Deut. 27:14–26). The carrying out of this proclamation of the law to the whole people, gathered in two groups on two mountains, is recounted in the book of Joshua, 8:30–35.

The efficacious word of the prophets takes on a new resonance within this scheme of the alliance. They denounce infidelity to the clauses of the alliance and point to its consequences. A curse will come down on those who do not pay heed to the word of the Lord, continually restated by his servants, the prophets. This is reasserted by Jeremiah, one of the prophets of the Deuteronomic reform, in his famous discourse against the temple in Jerusalem: 'If you will not listen to me . . . by paying attention to the words of my servants the prophets whom I so persistently send to you, without your ever listening to them, I will treat this temple as I treated Shiloh, and make this city a curse for all the nations of the earth' (Jer. 25:5–6; cf. 7:12–14). This is echoed by the prophet Malachi who tells the priests who are unfaithful to the alliance requirements regarding worship: 'If you do not listen . . . I will send the curse on you and curse your very blessing. Indeed I have already cursed it, since there is not a single one of you who takes this to heart' (Mal. 2:2).

A witness to the persistence of this concept of blessing and cursing in the framework of the alliance is provided by the text of a rule in the Qumran community. At the annual festival of renewal of the pact, there is provision for the priests to proclaim the formulae of blessing, with their cursing doublets, at the end of which all those who have gone through the pact ceremony reply, 'Amen, Amen' (1QS II; 1–18).

This examination of the OT texts concerning the efficacy of the word has shown particular features belonging specifically to the religious experience of Israel. While the concept of the operative efficacy of the word is shared with the cultures of surrounding peoples and forms part of their magical view of the world, it is also true that in the biblical context the effective word is closely linked to the image of God, creator of the world and Lord of history. His word is radically effective because it both expresses and actualises his power. The effective word of his mediators, priests and prophets, belongs to the same framework. This religious context is confirmed in the alliance, whose expression is through words of blessing and cursing with their effect for life or death, bringing happiness or ruin, expressing and actualising the power of God, Lord of history. But his is a power that includes the connotation of faithfulness, in which the members of the people of the alliance are also bound up. In such situations, the words of blessing or cursing, pronounced as a result of either fidelity or infidelity, express the extreme seriousness of man's relationship with God.

2. THE EFFECTIVE WORD IN THE NT

The experience described in the texts that make up the Christian canon basically follows the biblical mould, though with Judaic and Greek-Hellenistic influences that should be borne in mind. In fact Christians, to whom the writings of the NT are addressed, read the Bible in the Greek version prepared in the Hebrew colony of Alexandria. But the novelty of the Christian movement, compared to other Judaic reform groups of the first century, is contained in its relationship to Jesus of Nazareth, recognised and proclaimed as Christ and Lord. In the common evangelical tradition he is presented as a prophetic figure, distinguished by his healing activities and the efficacy of his word, both placed at the service of the announcement of the Kingdom of God. Some of his disciples, seen as the historical heads and founders of the new community in Palestine and throughout the Jewish Diaspora, are shown in the same light. Research should therefore take account of this double level and context, even though the actual texts in fact reflect the life experiences of the Christian communities to whom they were addressed.

(a) The Effective Word of Jesus

In the common synoptic tradition Jesus of Nazareth is shown in his public role as a charismatic and healing leader. The evangelist Mark makes this comment in his account of the beginning of his ministry in Capernaum: 'And his teaching made a deep impression on them because, unlike the scribes, he taught with authority' (Greek *exousia*) (Mark 1:22). And after giving a traditional literary account of the exorcism carried out by Jesus in the synagogue, he points up the reaction of the people present in these words: 'The people were so astonished that they started asking each other what it all meant. "Here is a teaching that is new," they said "and with authority behind it: he gives orders even to unclean spirits and they obey him"' (1:27). Matthew adds the same note at the end of the programmatic discourse to the disciples and the crowds on the mountainside (Matt. 7:28–29). But in this case the reference is not to the power of Jesus' word controlling and vanquishing the competing power of unclean spirits.

The first evangelist is perhaps amplifying and clarifying one of Mark's little summaries, placed in the same context of the day at Capernaum, concerning Jesus' effective exorcism: 'That evening they brought him many who were possessed by devils. He cast out the spirits *with a word* and cured all who were sick' (Matt. 8:16; see Mark 1:32–34). The third evangelist, Luke, follows Mark's text more closely in this instance. At the end of his account of the exorcism at Capernaum, he embellishes and clarifies Mark's comment in this form: 'Astonishment seized them and they were all saying to one another, "What teaching! He gives orders to unclean spirits with authority and power (Gr. *exousia-dýnamis*) and they come out"' (Luke 4:36; cf. 4:32).

This emphasis on the *exousia* and *dýnamis* of Jesus' word over the spirits corresponds to Luke's view, taking up a common feature of the synoptic tradition, of the personality of Jesus as manifesting an extraordinary power which places him, though in an exceptional and unique way, in the line of prophets called by God. The two disciples at Emmaus sum up their impressions of the figure of Jesus in these words: 'Jesus of Nazareth . . . proved he was a great (Gr. *dynatós*) prophet by the things he said and did in the sight of God and of the whole people' (Luke 24:19; see Acts 7:22).

The power of Jesus' word is expressed in a particularly impressive way in his healings, especially in his casting out of spirits. The double tradition of Luke and Matthew, in the account of Jesus' debate with the pharisees and scribes on the meaning of his exorcisms, records this *logion*: 'But if it is through the finger of God that I cast out devils, then know that the Kingdom of God has overtaken you' (Luke 11:20). Matthew retouches the image of 'finger of God', substituting 'spirit of God' (12:28). But both express the idea that Jesus' effective cures show forth and already bring about the liberating power of God who forces the power of Satan to recede. This is shown in the simile that follows immediately: that of the strong man guarding his palace, till a stronger man comes along, defeats him and shares out his spoil (Luke 11:21–22; Matt. 12:29–30). So in the synoptic tradition, the prodigious feats performed by Jesus during his travels in Galilee are called 'mighty works' (Gr. *dynámeis*) (Matt. 11:21; Luke 10:13). This is the public image of Jesus recorded by Mark and Matthew at the beginning of the scene in Nazareth, where those who are listening to him in the synagogue are astonished and ask: 'Where did this man get all this? What is the wisdom given to him? What mighty works (Gr. *dynámeis*) are wrought by his hands' (Mark 6:2; see 6:14). If the *dýnamis* of Jesus is shown in his healing acts, the power of his word is seen in an impressive way in the exorcisms. In the synoptic tradition there is not always a clear distinction made between healing and exorcism. So there is a tendency to recount some cases of healing as casting out of devils, and also to project the formulae of exorcism on to liberating gestures such as the calming of the storm (Mark 1:25; 4:39). The predilection for this literary form is probably due to Mark's desire to show the power and efficacy of Jesus' word.

This emerges clearly and typically in the account of the Gerasene demoniac, recounted in all three synoptic gospels. But Mark's version, within the form of exorcism, lays heightened stress on the contrast between the dehumanising power of the unclean spirits, which completely dominate the man and force him to live in the tombs, in the realm of death, and the power of Jesus' word. While respecting the literary form of an exorcism account, the gospel narrative places the liberating power of Jesus through his word in the forefront.[4] The evil spirit sees the presence of Jesus as a threat and tries to counter it through using his knowledge of Jesus' mysterious identity: 'What do you want with me, Jesus, son of the Most High God? Swear by God you will not torture me!' (Mark 5:6). But Jesus through his words regains the initiative by forcing the possessing spirit to reveal his identity: ' "What is your name?" Jesus asked. "My name is legion" he answered "for there are many of us" ' (5:9). Despite its expedient of the pigs, the demonic power, strong and organised at the beginning, ends up put to flight, drowned in the lake. Luke's version explicitates the symbolic value of this detail by making the devils plead with Jesus not to make them go down into the 'Abyss' (Gr. *abýssos*, Luke 8:31).

The efficacy of Jesus' word is again shown in another account of exorcism given in the common synoptic tradition after the transfiguration. The disciples have been unable to cure a poor boy possessed by 'a dumb spirit' (but who seems, from the gospel narrative, to have been suffering from epilepsy). His despairing father is insistent that Jesus come and intervene. 'And when Jesus saw how many people were pressing round him, he rebuked the unclean spirit.

"Deaf and dumb spirit," he said "I command you: come out of him and never enter him again" ' (Mark 9:25). Jesus' word is immediately effective. Then, when his disciples ask him privately why they were unable to cast it out, Jesus tells them, in both Mark and Matthew's account, of the need for strong faith expressed in effective prayer: 'This is the kind that can only be driven out with prayer' (Mark 9:29).

A similar lesson is taught in the only gospel episode in which the power of Jesus' word is expressed and shown in a curse: the barren fig tree. The episode is told by Mark and Matthew and there is an echo of this tradition in the third gospel in the parable of the barren fig tree, Luke 13:6–9. The episode forms part of Jesus' activities in Jerusalem, after his messianic entry which ended in the temple. The next day, leaving Bethany with his disciples, Jesus looks for fruit on a fig tree in leaf, but finds none. Then he says, 'May no one ever eat fruit from you again' (Mark 11:14). Matthew makes the effect follow immediately on the word, so that the disciples are amazed. Mark, however, inserts the episode of the expulsion of the dealers from the temple between the words of cursing and their producing an effect (11:15–19). In this way the symbolic allusion in Jesus' word-action is brought to the fore. His prophetic word points to the barrenness of Israel and proclaims the consequent curse according to the terms of the alliance. Mark tells that on the following day they went past the place and found the fig tree withered, Peter points this out to Jesus, which occasions the discourse on effective prayer (Mark 11:20–24; Matt. 21:20–22). This ecclesial recounting of the effective words of Jesus is interesting, in that it leaves us with the basic image of Jesus as one who denounces the faithlessness of Israel in the style of the prophets. In confirmation of this comes the series of 'woes' reproduced in different ways in the evangelical tradition, as in Matt. 23:13–32 and Luke 6:24–26.

(b) The Effective Word of the Disciples

This evangelical interpretation of Jesus as mighty in word and deed allows an insight into the concerns of the early community, which kept the tradition. A more direct verification, however, can be made by comparing the gospels with the letters of Paul. In reality, Paul, as far as can be seen from his surviving writings, shows no particular interest in the spiritual manifestations that may in some way be associated with effective or powerful words, working for good or ill. It is true that in his letters he alludes to the effectiveness of his mission, carried out by 'what I have said and done by the power of signs and wonders, by the power of the Holy Spirit' (Rom. 15:19; see 1 Cor. 2:4; 1 Thess. 1:5). Faced with those who question his authority as an apostle at Corinth, he points to the 'signs, the marvels, the miracles' (2 Cor. 12:12) that have accompanied his apostolic ministry. But in Paul's judgment there are not the signs or credentials of the true apostle. So he is diffident towards those who value these phenomena and use the word as an autonomous force. If he has recourse a couple of times to formulae of cursing, he does so spontaneously, following a Judaic manner of thought and expression, though in a Christian context and with Christian intention (Gal. 1:8–9; 1 Cor. 16:22). The operative efficacy of Paul's word is essentially linked to the *dýnamis* of the Gospel, working for the salvation of those who believe it (Rom. 1:16). The Gospel, as the public proclamation of Christ, is the 'sweet smell of life' for those who are being saved, but 'the smell of death' for those who are not (2 Cor. 2:15–16).

It is perhaps the second volume of Luke's work, the Acts of the Apostles, that best preserves the image of the disciples, who, in their activity of witness, strengthened by the power (*dýnamis*) of the Spirit, not only proclaim the word effectively, but in some way personify its power. In the community of Jerusalem, the model and prototype of the other communities, Peter unmasks the plot of the couple Ananias and Sapphira, who had yielded to Satan's tempting and kept back for themselves part of the money destined for the common coffers of the community. Doing this, Peter says, is lying not to men, but to God and to his Holy Spirit. Peter's words, which uncover this offence to the holy community, at the same time bring about a curse on those who place themselves beyond its rules (Acts 5:1–11). The case of Simon, the magician of Samaria, is analogous: impressed by the wonders that he saw worked by the Holy Spirit, carried out through the laying on of hands by Peter and John, he wished to share in that power (*exousía*). Peter denounces this perverse attempt in prophetic terms and tells him the ruin that will fall on him because his heart is warped. In the end Simon begs: 'Pray to the Lord for me yourselves that none of the things you have spoken about may happen to me' (Acts 8:18–24).

Alongside the picture of Peter operating in Jerusalem and the surrounding territory of Palestine, the author of Acts builds up one of Paul, the missionary called by the risen Christ and empowered by the Spirit to carry the word to kings and peoples. On the first mission outside Palestine, Paul, accompanied by Barnabas, went to Paphos in the island of Cyprus, where they came into contact with a Jewish magician and false prophet called Bar-Jesus, who was an attendant of the proconsul Sergius Paulus. This magician tried to stop them preaching the word of God to the proconsul, who had asked to hear them. Then Paul 'looked him full in the face' and denounced him as a false prophet 'twisting the straightforward ways of the Lord' and told him: 'Now watch how the hands of the Lord will strike you: you will be blind and for a time you will not see the sun' (Acts 13:11–12). And 'that instant', Acts goes on to say, 'everything went misty and dark for him'. The purpose of the author of Acts in this passage is to emphasise the power of the word proclaimed by Paul, which on the one hand unmasks the tricks of magical and syncretist opposition and on the other fulfils the positive expectations of those to whom it is addressed. The incident at Philippi, where Paul's efficacious word, following the gospel model, frees a young slave-girl from the spirit of soothsaying, is on the same lines (Acts 16:16–18).

These passages from the Acts of the Apostles show Luke's view of the efficacy of the word, which, following the prophetic model in the Bible, contains in itself a dynamism of salvation or damnation, in which its historical mediators, the apostles and other missionaries, participate. In other texts of the Christian tradition too, particularly those of an apocalyptic nature, there is a continuation of this concept of the effective word, by which judgment is carried out on evil, denouncing it and annihilating it at once. This is particularly so in the case of the protagonist of the last judgment, as expressed in 2 Thess. 2:8 and Rev. 19:11–12.

According to the NT witness, the effective words of Jesus and his disciples are set in the context of their mission or role in the service of the Kingdom of God or the Good News of salvation. This is the feature that distinguishes them from surrounding religious and cultural models, where the effective world was placed within the realm of magic. Jesus' word reveals and actualises the creative power of God who liberates and reintegrates man in his dignity. His words of denunciation in the form of 'cursing' carry on those of the prophets and definitively anticipate the final judgment God will pronounce on evil and death. The disciples, as his chosen ones and witnesses, share in this liberating and judging power of the word that denounces evil and proclaims the good of salvation.

Translated by Paul Burns

Notes

1. V. Mannucci *Bibbia come parola di Dio* (Brescia 1981) pp. 15–18.

2. The first tablet of the Babylonian creation poem which takes its name from its opening words *Enūma elish*, begins like this: 'When in the heights the heaven was not yet named / and the firm earth below had no name . . . when none of the gods existed / they had not been called by name / their fates had not been fixed / then gods were procreated in the midst of them / Lahmu and Lahamu came into existence / with a name they were called' (I, 1–10, in J. B. Pritchard *Ancient Near East Texts* (Princeton 1955) pp. 60–61); see Gen. 2:4b–7.

3. In the text of Numbers, Balaam is associated with the region of Pethor, on the river Euphrates, known in Assyrian texts as Pithru, and placed by Deut. 23:5 in Aram of the two rivers, between Syria and southern Mesopotamia. Confirmation of this setting comes from the second geographical reference in Numbers, 'in the land of the sons of Amaw', a name mentioned in cuneiform texts, whose land lay between Aleppo and Carchemish.

4. J. M. Hull *Hellenistic Magic and the Synoptic Tradition* (London 1974) pp. 61–72.

David Power

On Blessing Things

SINCE IT is impossible in one article to give a survey of the whole tradition of ecclesiastical blessings, attention is given in this essay to the blessing of things. It is hoped that in this way the meaning and intent of blessings will be illustrated and insight given into the issues of power. Some later articles in this number offer considerations on the blessing of baptismal waters and on the ritual. Here blessings are considered as a fact of daily life, with an eye to those blessings that are given outside a distinctively liturgical context, e.g. at a meal, or to the blessing of objects intended for use in daily life, e.g. oil, water, fruits, scapulars.

Studies on the Eucharist in recent decades have drawn attention to the Jewish *berakah* or blessing prayer. As a result, there is a tendency to model all Christian blessings on it and to emphasise the note of thanksgiving or praise addressed to God in blessings. On the other hand, there is a persistent demand on the part of the faithful to have things blessed in order to plead divine protection. This can even lead to a tension between an official mentality and a popular mentality on blessings. When the Paschal Vigil was restored in the fifties, the blessing of homes and food-stuffs that used to take place in some countries on Holy Saturday was put off until some day in the paschal season. Priests doing their rounds after Easter found that the people's disappointment over the failure to have their Easter table blessed greatly tempered the welcome given to them. One could multiply examples of this sort to show how in blessings people find a source of divine power, a mediation of good health, peace, favour, and safeguard against evil, which is more readily captured in an invocation of God's name over an object, or in a gesture such as the sign of the cross, than in an act of thanksgiving or of praise. Does this necessarily denote superstition? Is the emphasis on praise and thanksgiving imposed by ecclesiastical tradition? What is to be said from tradition about connections between human energy, demonic energy and divine energy, to which blessings are addressed?

1. HISTORICAL SURVEY: EARLY CENTURIES

The precise relation of Christian blessings to Jewish blessings is unclear, partly because of uncertainties in our knowledge of the Jewish tradition, partly because of obscurities in the Christian. Discussions over the *berakah*[1] are too many to rehearse here. Suffice to recall that Joseph Heinemann, who notes the dominance of the motif of praise in Jewish blessings, also notes the recurrence of the invocation of divine power. Thus of the daily *Tefillah* or eighteen blessings he writes:

> The principal content and purpose of these blessings is to give praise and thanks to God for the abundant goodness which he has bestowed upon his creatures and, at the same time, to obtain permission from him to enjoy the fruits of this world, for 'the earth is the Lord's, and the fulness thereof'. On the other hand, most of the eighteen benedictions . . . are petitionary in content. To be sure, each of these petitionary prayers concludes with a eulogy formula, and is thereby infused with elements of thanksgiving and praise to him who satisfies the needs of all his creatures . . . Nonetheless, the primary purpose of the weekday *Tefillah* is unquestionably to petition for Israel's necessities out of the firm conviction that the Lord will hear these supplications and respond favourably to them.[2]

While this is said of blessings for the people, it denotes the general sense of all blessings in Israel at the time of Christ and of the early Christian church. The interweaving of praise, thanksgiving and petition carries over into the Christian tradition.

(a) Eucharist, Eulogy

When turning to blessings over things as practised in the early Church, attention is first given to two blessings pronounced in the course of a meal, whose sacramental meaning is often discussed. These are the prayer over the bread and the prayer over the cup found in the ninth chapter of the *Didaché*.[3] Leaving aside the issue of their relation to the celebration of the Lord's Supper, these prayers can certainly be taken as paradigmatic of the blessing of things in an early Christian tradition, still much under the influence of Judaism. The blessing over the bread reads:

> We thank you, Father, for the life and knowledge which you have revealed to us through Jesus Christ your child. Glory to you through all ages.

In this Christian form of blessing, it is the thanksgiving motif rather than that of praise which is chosen, though the eulogy or praise at the end is typically Jewish. The object of the blessing is the life and knowledge given in Jesus Christ, rather than the divine providence evidenced in the produce of the bread from the fields, as accented in Jewish table-blessings. In the blessing of the cup at the end of the meal, one notes the invocation of the name of Jesus Christ. This is the Christian turn given to the invocation of the divine name found in Jewish traditions, an invocation which expresses both awe of the divine mystery and expectation of divine care.

In the two blessings from the *Didaché*, while they are pronounced over bread and wine to be shared in the fellowship, little is said of the significance of bread and wine in themselves, since all attention is given to the share in the blessings of Christ which the table mediates. This should not lead us to think that early Christians had no mind for the provident attention given to the production of earthly fruits. A good example of this is found in the blessing of first-fruits found in the *Apostolic Tradition*. Though the prayer begins with a formula 'We thank you, God', the body of the prayer is a eulogy or praise for God's action in creation and providence:

> Through your word you have made them grow; you have commanded the earth to bear all its fruits for the joy and nourishment of humanity and all the animals. For all this we praise you, O God, and for all the blessings you give us when you adorn the whole creation with all kinds of fruits, through your child, Jesus Christ, our Lord.[4]

In the lucernary, or blessing of light at the beginning of the evening meal, it is the motif of thanksgiving for the benefits of redemption which is developed. Picking up on the natural symbolism of light, the prayer then celebrates the gifts of redemption through an extension of this symbolism, referring it to Jesus Christ.[5]

If only the form of blessing is taken into account, one could say that in these two texts we have an example of a difference between a eucharist or thanksgiving, and a eulogy or praise. However, when the compiler of the *Apostolic Tradition* makes a distinction between a *eucharistia* and a *eulogia* he does not seem to have this in mind.[6] He uses the former term to signify either the prayer said at the celebration of the Lord's Supper, or the bread and wine which, being blessed, become the body and blood of Christ. *Eulogia* is then used to designate the prayer said by the bishop over the bread blessed at the beginning of a common meal or over the first-fruits and flowers which the people offer, or the bread and fruits which when blessed are shared.[7]

According to this distinction, where the intention is to distinguish all else from the sacrament of the Eucharist, the thanksgiving for the evening light would be classed as a eulogy, despite the etymological sense of praise attached to this word. This would lead to the conclusion that prayers of blessing over objects developed either in the form of thanksgiving or in the form of praise. From the two examples given from the *Apostolic Tradition*, one gets the impression that sentiments of praise dominated when thought was given to the works of creation, whereas thanksgiving prevailed in considering the work of redemption, though this is not to be taken as a hard and fast distinction.[8]

(b) Eulogy, Exorcism

It would also seem that in some cases eulogy had associations with the invocation of the divine name over objects, an invocation which amounted to a petition for the mediation of divine blessings or divine protection to those using the objects. This sense of blessing is found particularly in the East Syriac tradition and a good example is to be had in the *Acts of Thomas*.[9] It is disputed whether this blessing of bread is a Eucharist in the Lord's body. Whatever about this discussion, the prayer has its origins in the Jewish blessing of bread at the beginning of a meal and seems to give evidence of the Syrian Christian tendency to convert this blessing into an invocation of the divine name. The text is here quoted from an early Greek translation, rather than from the extant Syriac, since the latter seems to have been corrupted by later 'orthodox' interferences with the textual tradition:

> Bread of life, those who eat of which remain incorruptible: bread which fills hungry souls with its blessing—thou art the one to receive a gift, that thou mayest become for us forgiveness of sins, and they who eat thee become immortal. We name over thee the name of the mother of the ineffable mystery of the hidden powers and dominions, we name over thee the name of Jesus. May the power of this blessing (*eulogia*) come and remain in this bread so that souls who receive it may be washed of their faults.[10]

In this text, it is clear that the bread blessed is intended to mediate divine blessings upon those who eat it, particularly the forgiveness of sins and immortality. While this, of course, takes on particular significance if what is intended is the sacrament of the Eucharist, in a more general sense it reflects the power of *exorcism*, that is to say, the protection against the ills of body and spirit which is mediated through a share in blessed things. It is also to be noted that the core of the prayer is an invocation of the name. This invocation would seem to mix the name of the Spirit (the mother of the ineffable mystery) with the name of Jesus, reflecting an early East Syriac inclination to blur the distinction between Christ and the Holy Spirit. In any case, it has been suggested that the root of this blessing is the invocation of the divine name in Jewish prayers of which the most important is that said over Jerusalem in the daily synagogue prayer or *Tefillah*.

Some items about blessings in the *Apostolic Tradition* bear comparison with this exorcism or invocation of the divine name for care and protection against evil. For example, while the blessed bread given to the baptised at the end of a *synaxis* is called a eulogy, the bread given to the catechumens is called an exorcised bread.[11] As the name given to the bread for the baptised derives from the type of prayer said over it, so the bread given to the catechumens is probably derived from the type of prayer pronounced over it. The bread thus blessed was intended to mediate to the catechumens the divine power which they needed in their combats against Satan.

Though the word *exorcism* does not recur, the sense that things can mediate protection against ills of mind and body does crop up in the blessings of oil, cheese, olives and water. While the rubric or directive for the blessing of oil, cheese and olives says that the bishop is to give thanks over them in a prayer similar to the eucharistic *anaphora*, the compiler actually furnishes a text which constitutes a request for the solace and health of those who use the objects. The prayer develops a redemptive symbolism from the natural symbolism of the things themselves:

> O God, in making this oil holy thou givest holiness to those who use it and who receive it. Through it thou didst confer anointing on kings, priests and prophets. Let it procure likewise consolation for those who taste it and health for those who make use of it.[12]
>
> Make this curdled milk holy by uniting us to thy charity. Let this fruit of the olive never lose its sweetness. It is the symbol of the abundance which thou hast made to flow from the tree (of the Cross) for all those who hope in thee.[13]

The note of exorcism, with more attention than in the *Apostolic Tradition* or the *Acts of Thomas* to demonic powers, is highly developed in the blessings of oil and water at the end of the Sunday synaxis in the *Euchology of Serapion of Thmuis*:[14]

In the name of your only-begotten Son, Jesus Christ, we bless these creatures. We invoke the name of him who suffered, who was crucified, who rose from the dead and sits at the right hand of the Eternal, on this water and oil. Give these creatures the power to heal, let them drive out every fever, every demon and every sickness. Let them become for those who use them a healing and reviving remedy, in the name of your only-begotten Son, Jesus Christ. Through him, glory to you and power, in the Holy Spirit, now and for ever and ever. Amen.

Of this prayer, several things may be noted. First of all, it is a blessing in the form of an invocation of the divine name, revealed to us anew in Jesus Christ. Secondly, it is a petition for divine power, a power that is invoked indeed over material things, but that is mediated through them to human beings. Thirdly, it expresses the feeling that all of human life is affected by the redemption, so that people may pray for health of body as readily as they may ask for forgiveness of sins and grace. Fourthly, the prayer closes with the doxology customary to other forms of blessing. Fifthly, and perhaps most significantly, in developing the imagery of the demonic the text conjures a sense that all creation is caught in a struggle between demonic powers and the divine power that saves and redeems.

Peter Brown sees this sort of consciousness of the demonic as something which came to the fore in the third century, rather than as something to be found in earliest times. He writes:

Men who had discovered some inner perfection in themselves, who felt capable of intimate contact with the One God, found the problem of evil to be more intimate, more drastic. To 'look at the sum total of things', to treat human miseries with detachment—as so many regrettable traffic-accidents on the well-regulated system of the universe—was plainly insufficient. It made no sense of the vigour of conflicting emotions within oneself. Hence the most crucial development of these centuries: the definitive splitting off of the 'demons' as active forces of evil, against whom men had to pit themselves. . . .[15]

At the same time, the author notes, these demonic powers, all-embracing agents of evil in the affairs of the human race, were held in check by the divine power mediated through the community, especially through the agency of holy persons.[16] The exorcism pronounced over objects to be used by the faithful seems to have been part of this check, assurance of a divine protection and deliverance. The exorcism of early prayers, it will be noted, is not intended to free things themselves from demonic control, but to free the humans who use them in their daily life as a kind of sacramental mediation.

Offering

A survey of early Christian blessings would be incomplete if note were not taken of the fact that offering is at times associated with them. In the *Apostolic Tradition*, the oil, olives, cheese, flowers and fruit blessed by the bishop are offered by the faithful.[17] It is also said that when the bishop says the eulogy over things, he offers them,[18] while on the other hand the thanksgiving over the light is apparently not understood to constitute an offering.[19]

The language of offering in the early Church was polyvalent, and is therefore at times obscure to contemporary readers. It was a matter of assuming the language of offering and sacrifice into a way of life and of worship wherein the accent was on growth in the Spirit and upon the gifts that God gives. To call the bishop's blessing an offering is in line with the notion that Christian prayer, especially that of praise and thanksgiving, is a new form of cult, constituting in itself a spiritual offering. For the people to offer things of the earth (which were then going to be used by them at home or shared in community) was to adopt an old covenant perception of first-fruits as offerings to be made to God within a Christian context. This offering symbolised acknowledgment that all good things come from God, as well as the hope that God through provident care would attend to the health of mind and body of those who believe in Jesus Christ as redeemer, the one in whom the whole of creation is recapitulated, to use the imagery of Irenaeus.

Conclusions

This fairly summary sketch of blessings in early Christian centuries allows us to draw some conclusions. First of all, we find that three forms of prayer were in vogue, namely, acts of *thanksgiving* over the goods of creation which focussed on their redemptive symbolism, acts of *praise* which expressed wonder at the providence of God manifested in the fruits of the earth as well as a sense of reverence in their use, and acts of *petition*, invoking the divine name or divine power on things, so that they might serve to mediate divine care and divine protection to those who used them. This distinction is based on the historical evidence, but is not to be taken too rigorously, since any prayer could include all three forms or any one or two of them.

Secondly, we can note how the earth and its fruits were increasingly looked upon in redemptive perspective. While one might be inclined to say that they represented God's creative power, Christians saw the whole world and humanity's relation to it within the horizon of Christ's redemption, or recapitulation.

In the third place, invocation of divine power over things for the sake of those who use them, was as much a part of an early blessing tradition as was thanksgiving. This did not reflect a separation of the sacred from the profane, nor the idea that things blessed were sacralised. Rather did it reflect an understanding of sacramental power, that is, the sense that redemption included all creation and that through the things of daily life God mediates protection and love.

In the fourth place, it seems that the request for divine mediation was gradually developed in terms of the need for protection against demonic powers. The idea was not that Satan had power over the things of the earth, but that the human persons who made use of them could be subject to Satan. Apparently it was felt that God was so close to creatures in the good things of the earth, so provident of them, that protection against Satan might well be mediated through this agency.

Fifthly, all blessings from this age have fundamentally that significance which is rooted in the eucharistic blessing, namely, that all things are redeemed in Christ and that in all the uses of the things of this earth believers share in the grace and goodness of the redemption.[20]

Finally, account has to be taken of the action of holy persons or charismatics in giving blessings. The texts that we have are found largely in canonical collections and so reflect what was done in assemblies, the prayer given by the bishop. However, this should not cloud the fact that divine power was thought to be mediated through persons rather than through formulas, however well constructed. One would have to pursue the investigation further to show that the role of charismatics in blessings and healings, the recourse to hermits against the powers of devils, are an integral part of the history of blessings in the early Christian centuries. In any case, we have to remember that in the ordination tradition of the time it was a holy person who was sought out for the office of bishop, so that there was no danger of isolating his role in the community from the power of his prayer before God or from his power as a person to mediate divine blessings. Activity in prayer was grounded in a sense of the Christian person as mediator of God's blessings, and only secondarily in the mediation of office as such.

2. THE MEDIEVAL WORLD

(a) The Multiplication of Blessings

Peter Brown in his work on late antiquity notes that between the sixth and ninth centuries less attention was given to the blessings mediated by holy persons and more to the holy things themselves as agents of protection, or images of divine presence. The holy things made God visible or tangible and conveyed the patronage of the saints to whom they were dedicated.[21] Along with this went an increasing accent on exorcism, not now simply in the sense that through blessed objects God would give love and care to their users, but more and more in the sense that things themselves had to be rescued from Satan's power.

In his work on blessings, A. Franz has given many examples of the blessing of things in the middle ages.[22] Rituals and Pontificals reflect a growing concern with the subjection of the world to the demonic. The increasing number of exorcisms in the form of exsufflation of devils shows more interest in the safeguard from evil than in the sharing between Christians of divine graces. The tendency is then to attach a blessing, completed often by and exorcism, to everything. The *benedictio ad omnia* is typical of the medieval ages. Though rituals supply innumerable blessings for things in the home and things in the fields or other places of work, this blessing provides for the unforeseen occasion, when a specific blessing is wanting.

As a principle of interpretation, one should note that the meaning of blessings cannot be derived from the texts alone. One has to imagine the world which is reflected in such an abundant collection of exorcisms and blessings. For example, the text of the *benedictio ad omnia*, preserved from medieval texts in the 1614 Roman Ritual, is very close in terms to early church blessings. Through an invocation of the divine name, the prayer asks for the health of mind and body of those who will use the blessed object. However, the very existence of such a blessing, alongside many specific blessings, for such things as cornfields, granaries, kitchens, pots and pans, as well as the increasing need for exorcism and protection against the devil, suggests the transactions (spiritual and no doubt monetary) that went on between people and priests. The people seem to have prevailed upon priests to invoke God's name frequently over domestic and utility objects, as well as over objects of devotion that would serve as guarantees of divine surveillance or heavenly patronage. The actual words of blessing may often have mattered little, more merit being attached to physical acts, such as the sign of the cross or an oral exsufflation of the devil.

(b) The Blessing of Water

The blessing of water obtained increasing importance in the medieval world. Like the *benedictio ad omnia* it was something that provided for all necessities. With blessed water on hand, people had an ever-ready protection against sickness and other kinds of evil, and a constant agent of God's care to be sprinkled on whoever or whatever stood in need.

The text of the blessing of water, destined for sprinkling in the home, that is found in the Gelasian Sacramentary, gives a good example of how the symbolism of water was developed. The idea behind the blessing is that the water may be used to protect homes against Satan. Old Testament episodes are evoked to convey this meaning. On the one hand, the water is likened to the blood of the Paschal lamb sprinkled on the door-posts of the Israelites prior to the exodus to protect them from the hand of the avenging angel. On the other hand, the water was apparently felt to have an ambiguous relation to God, since it had to be sweetened (by the infusion of salt), as Elijah sweetened the bitter waters with his axe-head.[23]

(c) Blessings and Saints

The importance of blessings given by holy persons in early Christian centuries has already been noted. However, as early as Paulinus of Nola Franz has indicated the connection made between blessed objects and saints.[24] Amongst other gifts, sent to his friends either with or for a blessing, Paulinus seems to have sent the relics of martyrs or other holy persons, with the intention of sharing together in the divine blessings evidenced in the life of the venerable deceased. Other examples are also given by Franz: the *Vita Severini* calls a relic *sancti Johannis Baptistae benedictio*, and Gregory the Great speaks of relics of Mark, Peter and Paul as *benedictiones*. Such usage probably derives from the practice of blessing these objects with a prayer that invoked the name of the saint. What we have in these examples is the fusion of devotion to martyrs or other holy deceased with the practice of sharing communion in an exchange of blessings, as well as with the practice of mediating divine power through whatever is blessed.

Throughout the middle ages, the cult of the saints intruded more and more on blessings. The martyr or saint took on the role of patron, that is, one who had the ear of God and could therefore exercise power and influence on behalf of devotees. Not only were relics blessed, but their use in blessings to touch people was a tangible guarantee of patronage and protection. It is not surprising that the Blessed Mary's patronage is often invoked in blessings and that special blessings were attached to a number of her feasts.

(d) Different Worlds?

One cannot look for an even and uniform development of blessings in the middle ages, for this would be to assume a logical, coherent and universally similar spirituality. Besides the blessings that emphasised the need for the protection of God's power against demonic power, there were those that accentuated the distinction between the profane and the holy. Already in the Gelasian Sacramentary, one finds that everything connected with public worship had to be blessed or consecrated.[25] Churches, altars, vestments and vessels for worship are all provided with blessings. The texts themselves are quite appealing, since they do not attach any specific power or holiness to the objects themselves but are concerned with priestly service in spirit and in truth. However, the withdrawal of things from profane usage, the Old Testament imagery of priestly cult, and the setting-off of the ecclesiastical world from the popular are significant factors in these blessings. Contemporary with the emergence of these specific blessings is the fact that all blessings seem to have become the preserve of priests, so that the power of the priest as such even intruded into the world of popular blessings. There were apparently two kinds of power recognised by the people, both of which they accommodated to their needs: the power of the holy person, now identified with the saints in heaven, and the power of priestly office. They had to be brought into league with one another, for the protection of the people in a world of woes and dangers.

Another kind of world is reflected in other blessings, of which a good example is the blessing of a knight's sword at his investiture, such as is found in the tenth century Romano-Germanic Pontifical.[26] This quite beautiful text belongs to that quest for lay spirituality which would allow lay persons their part in the conquest of the world for God in what had become a clerically and monastically dominated society.[27] The knightly or crusader spirituality was not the only one whereby people in those centuries sought their place in the kingdom of God, but it was one that allowed a lay person to claim a role as one who defends the kingdom against its enemies, tributary to other dominions, and as one who protects its most vulnerable members, the widow and the orphan. The blessing reads:

> Hear, Lord, our prayers, and with the power of your right hand bless this sword with which your servant wishes to gird himself. May he use it for the defence and protection of churches, of widows and orphans, and of all those who serve God, against the savagery of pagans. May it strike all those who attack your Church with fear and trembling.

The blessing ceremony included the singing of Psalm 45, with a special accent on verse 3: 'Strap your sword upon your thigh, O mighty warrior.'

From one point of view, this text might seem to reflect the subjection of the temporal to the spiritual order and the tendency of the Church to sanctify war when it seems to suit its own ambitions to power. From another point of view, however, it has to be seen in its own time as an attempt on the part of the laity to find their own due place in God's kingdom. The blessing was probably composed more as an accommodation of the clergy to the spiritual aspirations of the knightly class than as an attempt of clerics to arraign this class to their service. In a comparable category of blessings one would place that of the rough robes of the mendicants, for this would represent a kind of accommodation between clerical and monastic holiness, on the one hand, and that of the new order of those who sought holiness by an evangelical poverty in the world of the poor, on the other.

Careful attention, then, to the blessings of things that developed during the middle ages over a period of centuries reveals the, at times uncomfortable, accommodation of different worlds to one another. In the first place, there was the ecclesiastical world, in which the sacred was separated from the profane and cult imposed a special status on its practitioners. All the laity suited themselves to this world, by accepting that blessings had to be mediated through the agency of the clergy, even when some challenged the power of the clergy by demanding that the sanction of a holy life was required for the exercise of office. In the second place, there was the world of the more socially and politically powerful laity, who wanted to find their own place in God's reign and saw themselves particularly as its defenders against the onslaughts of the evil one. In the third place, there was the world of the common people, subject to dire necessity and to poverty, people often without protection or patronage against the uncertainties of nature or the exigencies of the powerful, a world wherein recourse to heavenly patronage and divine protection seemed the only viable safeguard. These three worlds interlocked and interplayed, but the people in them mapped their course by different charts.

3. THE POST-TRIDENTINE WORLD

In ecclesiastically approved rituals during the centuries that followed on the Council of Trent, it is the distinction between the sacred and the profane that seems to dominate the blessing of things. Whatever was to serve in the sacred order had to be withdrawn from the profane. Exorcisms are linked with blessings because things have to be wrested from the sway of the devil.[28]

At the same time, one has to note all during this period the devotion represented by the blessing and wearing of scapulars in honour of Mary and the saints, as well as other particular blessings such as that of the cords of Saint Philomena. Blessings of such objects as bread, wine or water in honour of a particular saint also continued, and the blessing of fields or fishing fleet could be done with great festivity.

Vestiges of this proliferation of blessings and blessed objects remain in the appendix of the 1614 *Roman Ritual* even after its revision in 1925, to meet the requirements of the 1917 code of canon law. The euchology of these blessings retains the ancient demand for *sanitas mentis et corporis*, but it accentuates the hope of heaven. To introduce the hope of heaven was the ecclesiastic's way of orienting the need for help in the world of the common people. The people might have recourse to blessings and blessed objects in a world of powerlessness, in the hope of a supernatural prevention of illness or of protection against impending calamities, or in the trust that God could dominate nature in such a way as to give them abundance of sea and harvest. The priests, however, possibly dreading the superstitious or ineffectual inclinations of such hopes, or fearing that dissatisfaction could lead to something more crass, directed the people's thoughts to heaven. The world could then be lived in, in the hope that God and heavenly patrons would assuage the necessities of this life, and in the knowledge that suffering endured would be merit for the joys of after-life.

4. REFLECTIONS

This short, and necessarily partial, survey of the history of the blessing of things gives rise to some reflections, pertinent to their form and usage today.

(a) Forms

In the canon of Church tradition, there is no stereotyped form of blessing, but from earliest times, as noted above, one finds a mixture of forms, inclusive of praise, thanksgiving, invocation of the divine name, exorcism, and even offering. In the early tradition, the underlying faith to which expression is given is that the whole world is suffused with divine power and all things and their usage are affected by God's creative and redemptive love. Later traditions, wherein protection against demonic power is the prevalent sentiment, or the patronage of saints is invoked against calamities, or the holy is separated from the profane, are departures from this early conviction.

(b) Eschatology

The tone and purpose of blessings necessarily change as a people's or an age's eschatological perspective changes. Early blessings belonged to the *eschaton* of the covenant community, which believed in the advent of God's reign, and sharing in natural things shared thereby in the divine blessings of creation and redemption. A later age was tributary to a world wherein all things were seen to be caught up in the combat between God and Satan, between the power of two kingdoms. There were different perspectives on this combat, the one seeing all things as corrupt and the other seeing them corrupted by human misuse. A vision of the universe that separates the sacred and the profane is still another perception of God's presence and power in the world, and many blessings belong within an eschatological view that life in this world is a time of suffering, preparatory to the hope of heaven.

(c) Interpretation

As already observed, blessings have to be interpreted not only according to the text but within the world to which those who transact them belong. It is quite possible for different persons to share the same ceremony with divergent meanings. Blessing is a transaction between persons and one has to ask what benefits the different parties deem themselves to derive, and what power they exercise over one another and over the things of God and the things of the earth. While in the medieval and modern worlds, the clergy have been acknowledged as the ones who mediate divine power, and the doctors and scribes who composed the texts appear to have had adequate knowledge of early traditions and euchology, one always has to ask how much it was the people who determined the field wherein these divine blessings were invoked. How much reflects the accommodation of ecclesiastical authority, with ambiguous intent, to people's demands upon them? How much reflects the compromise whereby priestly and ecclesiastical power could be held secure, even while allowing the people and their needs to set the agenda for devotion and blessing?

(d) Powerlessness

The relation of blessing to powerlessness and to the powerless seems to be one of the major factors to be taken into account in a proper understanding of the blessing of things. The fundamental meaning of blessing, whatever form it takes, is that God's power redeems the powerless. Earliest Christian communities, sects to the prevalent religious and temporal cultures of their time and place, could see themselves made powerful in Christ. They found their way of dwelling on earth and using among themselves the things of earth by reason of their strength in Christ. This depended on the strength of being a community in him. The community's protection of the widow and the orphan, that is of its own powerless, is a necessary underpinning to the praise of God and the invocation of the divine name over the things of the earth, which all shared in common.

Without the privilege and support of a close community, flung upon a world where they could have no earthly protection, the poor of later times had typical resort to heavenly patronage and to the hope of divine intervention. Even the more wealthy among Christians could lack the power that goes with status and dignity, so that they too had recourse to patronage and blessing. *Dignitas*, we know, was an important theme in early medieval Christianity and its influence on the fascination for the blessings given in honour of saints, looked upon as patrons, is not to be discounted.

It is, however, those who have little or no source of worldly power, whether of wealth or of dignity or of influence, who appear to have the most frequent recourse to blessings. Prelates and the new *kleros* of the educated often regard this interest in blessings as a superstition, or at least as prone to superstition, and there is no doubt that it has in places survived with little else left of Christian faith or practice.[29] This fear of superstition seems to be one of the reasons for the current trend to let the form of thanksgiving have pride of place in blessings, over petition or the invocation of God's name. However, one does not meet the reality simply by laying traps for superstition. Future development in the practice of blessing depends on how the Church sees the power of God to be given to the powerless of the earth. What kind of liberation does the Spirit of Christ bring to the helpless? What personal sense of power does the Gospel give them? The underpinning of community, with its corporate strength, will be necessary to such development. The language of their demands defines the world in which the poor live, bereft of power but possessing their own independence and dignity. This self-definition is to be respected, not tampered with.[30] Only if this language is comprehended, only if it can be expressed how God's power comes to people in a world defined by that language, will it emerge what it can mean to bless God in such a world, and what it means to invoke God's blessing.

Notes

1. See the article in this issue by J. M. R. Tillard, note 5.

2. Joseph Heinemann *Prayer in the Talmud: Forms and Patterns* (Berlin and New York 1977) p. 18.

3. *La Doctrine des douze apôtres* ed. W. Rordorf, Sources Chrétiennes 248 (Paris 1978). The English translation given here is taken from L. Deiss *Early Sources of the Liturgy* (London 1967) pp. 13–15.

4. *La Tradition apostolique* ed. B. Botte (Münster 1963) no. 31. The English translation is taken from Deiss, the work cited in note 3, at p. 67.

5. *Ibid*. no. 25.

6. *Ibid*. no. 26.

7. For a similar use of *eulogia* in a Latin text, see the journal of Aetheria: *Ethérie: journal de voyage* ed. H. Petre, Sources Chrétiennes 21 (Paris 1957) pp. 106/7, note 1.

8. According to Hippolytus, first-fruits and flowers were to be offered and blessed, but not vegetables. See no. 31.

9. On these blessings, see G. Rouwhorst 'Bénédiction, action de grâces, supplication: Les oraisons de la table dans le Judaïsme et les célébrations eucharistiques des Chrétiens syriaques' in *Questions liturgiques* 61 (1980) 211–240.

10. E. Hennecke and W. Schneemelcher *New Testament Apocrypha II*, translated by R. McWilson (London 1973) p. 427.

11. *Apostolic Tradition*, no. 26.

12. *Ibid*. no. 5f.

13. *Loc. cit.*

14. F. X. Funk *Didascalia et constitutiones apostolorum* II, (Paderborn 1905), pp. 158–194. The English text given here is taken from Deiss, the work cited in note 3, at p. 121.

15. Peter Brown *The World of Late Antiquity* (Singapore 1971) p. 53.

16. *Ibid*. 101.

17. *Apostolic Tradition*, no. 5f.

18. *Ibid*. no. 28.

19. *Ibid*. no. 27: 'He does not say: "Let us lift up our hearts" because that is said at the moment of the offering'. Above all, the author does not want anything else to be confused with the sacrament of the Lord's body and blood.

20. Tillard develops this thought in his article, appearing in this number of *Concilium*.

21. Brown, the work cited in note 15, at pp. 182–187.

22. A. Franz *Die kirchlichen Benediktionen im Mittelalter*, 2 vols. (Freiburg-im-Breisgau 1909). This remains the authoritative work on blessings.

23. *Liber sacramentorum romanae aeclesiae ordinis anni circuli* (*Sacramentarium Gelasianum*) ed. L. Mohlberg, nos. 1556–1557 (Rome 1960).

24. Franz, vol. 1, 239–246.

25. *Sacramentarium Gelasianum* pp. 689–702.

26. *Pontificale Romano-Germanicum* ed. C. Vogel and R. Elze, vol. 2 (Rome 1968) CCXLIV, p. 379.

27. See A. Vauchez *La spiritualité du moyen-âge occidental: VIIIe-XIIe siècles* (Paris 1975) pp. 65–74.

28. See A. Gignac 'Les Bénédictions: sous le signe de la création et de l'éspèrance évangelique' in J. Gelineau *Dans vos assemblées*, vol. 2 (Paris 1971) pp. 579–593.

29. For an interesting perspective on this, see Roger Bastide *The African Religions of Brazil: Toward a Sociology of the Interpretation of Civilizations* (Baltimore and London 1978) pp. 349–352.

30. Compare André Aubry 'The Feast of Peoples and the Explosion of Society—Popular Practice and Liturgical Practice' *Concilium* 142 (2/1981) (English Edition) p. 35.

PART II

The Blessing of Baptismal Waters: Comparative Liturgical Inquiry

Alex Stock

The Blessing of the Font in the Roman Liturgy

1. A RITE IN TRANSITION

THEOLOGY'S RELATIONSHIP to the blessing of the water used at baptism is rather tense. In the 1970 reform of the *Missale Romanum* this part of the Easter liturgy was changed so drastically that one is forced to recognise more than a mere cleaning up of the text's surface. What is involved is a profound structural change in the conception of blessing. This is confirmed if one also looks at the liturgical formulae for blessing the baptismal water to be found in the *Ordo baptismal parvulorum* and the *Ordo initiationis christianae adultorum* of the new Rituale Romanum, published in 1969 and 1972. The new title that was chosen in the former—*Benedictio et invocatio Dei super aquam*—provides a programmatic formulation of the tendency underlying the reform.[1] It lies in the semantic displacement of the word *benedictio* from actual blessing of the substance water to *benedictio Dei*, so that the blessing becomes a praising of God over the water.

Relatively controversial views about the genesis of this wished-for transformation and about how it took place appear in the discussion of the history of the rite of blessing the baptismal water, a discussion that developed an increasingly practical bent in the context of Vatican II. What was unanimous was the desire to shorten the rite and give it a clearer structure. If we look at the results of this reform the first thing to strike us is the marked pruning of ritual gestures. The previous rite was interwoven with a variety of gestures. After the reform the only one that is left is the plunging of the paschal candle into the water, and even this is made optional (*pro opportunitate*).

Already in the scholarly discussion far less attention was paid to the ritual gestures than to the texts. They were generally treated as secondary, both in the historical and in the logical sense: as later additional rites that were not always beneficial to the meaning of the text. Hence it is no wonder that the opportunity of getting rid of them was made use of. While just at this time avant-garde art was re-discovering the possibilities of expression through body language, the Church reformers obviously saw no opportunity for a positive and creative renewal of the inherited gestures. This is a remarkable phenomenon, and one worth thinking about. What it demonstrates, to begin with, quite independently of the possible meaning of the ritual gestures, is a process of disincarnation and dematerialisation of the liturgical action of blessing, balanced by giving it a verbal and spiritual emphasis. What is reflected in the withdrawal of gestures is the deliberate re-naming of the rite of the blessing of water, a change from a *benedictio aquae* that literally affects the water itself, to a *benedictio Dei* hovering over the water. What one could diagnose here is the Roman liturgy taking over in its own way and after a certain historical delay the general process of the disincarnation and dematerialisation of religion found in the modern age since the Reformation and the Enlightenment. But such a diagnosis remains far too sweeping without a critical discussion of the rites themselves.

2. A PHALLIC RITE?

In the new blessing of the font in the Easter Vigil all that remains of the previous gestures is the plunging of the paschal candle into the water, *pro opportunitate*. But even this rite has been modified. The previous rubrics laid down that the paschal candle was first to be dipped only a little way into the water, then deeper and finally right to the bottom, accompanied by the chant repeated three times each on a higher note: *Descendat in hanc plenitudinem fontis virtus Spiritus Sancti*, while after the final repetition the celebrant breathed on the water three times and concluded the chant with the words: *Totamque huius aquae substantiam regenerandi fecundet effectu*. In 1950 E. Stommel wrote of this ritual action that 'in its present form' it offers 'the impressive climax of the blessing of baptismal water. With reference to the art of liturgical expression and liturgical drama it deserves to be called one of the finest liturgical actions. It achieves this impression through the perfect combination of several liturgical artistic forms to produce a completely unified creation'.[2] This aesthetic quality cannot have been so obvious any longer to those responsible for deciding on liturgical reform. A number of changes were introduced into the rite. The dramatic formula of the *Descendat* was changed into a prayer with a trinitarian structure. The closing section with its mention of the water being fertilised was replaced by a text derived from Romans 6: *ut ommes, cum Christo consepulti per baptismum in mortem, ad vitam cum ipso resurgant.* The act of breathing on the water was removed. A single immersion was regarded as enough, and there was no longer any question of a climax created by the rise in pitch.

These changes affect precisely those aspects of the rite that according to E. Stommel were decisive for its aesthetic value. What then was the motive behind the reform? In the discussion of this rite in the context of liturgical history there is, despite all the other differences, unanimity in wanting to exclude one particular interpretation at all costs: that suggested by comparative religion to the effect that what we have here is a phallic fertility rite. From the point of view of the history of the liturgy it is pointed out that in the older sources there is mention not of one candle but of two or several. In other words, it seems to have been primarily a rite based on the practical necessity of providing adequate illumination for the font. On this practical basis a symbolic meaning would then have been built which represented the fertilisation as the flame coming down and illuminating the water, so that plunging the candle in more deeply would not mean anything in itself but merely be the means of bringing the flame as close as possible to the surface of the water so as to illuminate the whole of it.[3] This argument from the history of the liturgy is then supplemented by the argument based on theological principle 'that the fertilisation of the Church as a *virgo nesciens virum* like Mary could not be represented, even in the early years of the Church, by the symbol of human fertility. The spiritual nature of the Christian idea of God would not admit such a symbol of God's vivifying power into the framework of Christianity.'[4]

The framework of interpretation based on the virgin birth that is assumed in this line of argument admits at the most a hovering above and an illumination from without, but not a penetrating sexual symbol. Nevertheless the interpretation favoured by the liturgical experts did not in fact turn out to be so obvious as to be able to safeguard the aesthetic aspect of the rite in the course of reform. It was changed, with the explicit intention that 'the phallic misinterpretation (apparently justified by the previous text)' should be 'ruled out from the start'.[5]

3. THE DRAMA OF FERTILISATION

What is undisputed is that the texts of the old rite of the blessing of the baptismal water are concerned with fecundation. What is less clear is the relationship to them of the ritual gestures that are always classified as secondary. This link between 'myth' and 'rite' will become in what follows the guiding principle of a re-reading of the texts. The starting-point is that, however complicated the history of their origination may be, in their final form what we have is not an agglomeration of heterogeneous elements but the score of a coherent treatment of the mysteries. This can be checked by seeing if the gesture can be read as aspects of the ritual mimesis of a process of fertilisation.

In the first gesture the celebrant divides the water with the flat of his hand in the form of a cross. The gesture is embedded in the prayer that God will look upon the face of his Church and open the baptismal fountain so that it may accept the grace of the Holy Spirit: that is, that he will fertilise the water through the mysterious incorporation of his divintiy (*arcana sui numinis admixtione fecundet*) so that after receiving sanctification from the immaculate womb of the divine fountain (*sanctificatione concepta ab immaculato divini fontis utero*) a heavenly generation, born again as a new creature, may emerge. This first gesture of dividing the water has in the ritual drama of fecundation the function of disclosing the opening of the womb.

The second gesture consists of the water being moved with the hand. This gesture is embedded in an act of exorcism intended to protect the water from the influence of unclean spirits. In the opening of the fountain's womb lurks the danger that a door is being opened for all kinds of rival besiegers to invade by (*ab omni impugnatoris incursu*) and that hostile forces may involve themselves (*contrariae virtutis admixtio*). The font must be protected from this demoniac poisoning.

The third gesture is a threefold sign of the cross over the water. This gesture of blessing introduces a series of paradigms involving water which can be read 'here in the sense of a prescriptive proof of God's prior right to the possession and use of water against the claims of demons'.[6]

The recitation of the paradigm of the fountain of paradise is accompanied by a gesture in which the water is divided and sprinkled to the four corners of heaven. This fourth gesture is on the one hand the representation in gesture of the text being recited while on the other hand it refers back to the first opening division of the water where the accompanying text already spoke of the city of God being gladdened from this fountain and the peoples of the entire earth being renewed. In the liturgical action the baptismal font becomes the lifegiving core of the world.

The beginning of the series of paradigms involving water is recapitulated at the start of the New Testament section with a renewed *benedico te*: the threefold sign of the cross at the beginning is echoed by a single sign of the cross.

The sixth gesture that now follows consists of the water being breathed on three times in the form of a cross. The accompanying text interprets this breathing as an act of blessing (*benedictio*) to give the water the power to make clean. To this extent this ritual element recapitulates the exorcism theme of the banishing of unclean spirits. The form of the cross takes up the signs of the cross of the series of paradigms involving water: what had previously been represented manually is now recapitulated with an oral gesture.

There now follows the rite we have described above, the real significance of which is disputed: the *descendat* epiclesis with the plunging of the paschal candle into the water. After this the holy water (*aqua benedicta*) is sprinkled over the people and put aside for subsequent sprinklings.

But the rite as a whole is not over yet. A final complex of gestures involves the pouring in of the holy oils, first the oil of catechumens, then the chrism, then both oils together. Finally the celebrant mixes the oil with the water and divides it with his hand through the entire font. The three pourings correspond to the three plungings of the paschal candle. The text that accompanies the pouring in of the oil of catechumens says: *Sanctificetur et fecundetur fons iste oleo salutis renascentibus ex eo in vitam aeternam.* The two other pourings are accompanied by trinitarian formulae. It is only with this *commixtio* of the oil with the water of the baptismal font that the *arcana admixtio* prayed for at the beginning and the fecundation tied up with it find their liturgical completion. That ends the *benedictio aquae baptismalis.*

Conception and fertilisation is not the only theme that dominates the texts. It is represented mimetically in the form of a ritual drama in the succession of gestures and the texts accompanying them. The ancient world's ideas about the role of semen are given a symbolic re-working.[7] Certain recurrences are not to be seen as unnecessary repetitions but throughout correspond to the slow build-up of the proceedings. The complex of ritual that surrounds the plunging of the paschal candle into the water is the unmistakable climax of this drama. The rite does not distance itself from the material world through words, nor does it take the illumination of the water as the guiding clue of the representation: rather it does not shy away from touching the water with mouth and hands and from becoming physically involved with it. If we look at it without prejudice it is difficult in the context of the whole to see the plunging of the paschal candle into the water as other than a phallic role.

4. THE NEW RITE

The liturgical drama described in the previous section belongs to the past. The new rite of the blessing of the baptismal water during the Easter Vigil is substantially shorter and built up afresh by the use of old material. It has the form of a longer prayer with a final acclamation by the people. The prayer begins with a multiple invocation of God which through its collection of relative clauses alludes to a series of paradigms involving water from the Old and New Testaments. The prayer that follows has three sections. It asks for God to look upon the face of his Church and to open to it the fountain of baptism; for this water to receive the grace of the Holy Spirit; and for the power of the Holy Spirit to descend into this font. The new text refers back to the old (*Respice*, *Descendat*) but gives the material a thorough re-working. The theme of fecundation that dominated the old rite has been done away with as far as possible and replaced by the theme of resurrection. This leads to certain confusions of meaning. The Johannine rebirth from water and the Spirit is re-written to become a resurrection from water and the Spirit. And the coming down of the power of the Spirit is no longer meant to serve the fertilisation of the water but so that all who are buried with Christ in his death may be raised up to life with him. The theological insight based on Romans 6 that sees baptism in terms of being buried and raised up is inserted into a sentence that originally dealt with conception and fertilisation. In the pattern of *sepultura* and *resurrectio* the baptismal font can only take on the position of the *sepulcrum*—not the uterus that is to be impregnated. The blessing of the baptismal water had therefore to involve a symbolic representation of the font as a grave. One could link this with Christ's descent into hell and interrupt this as a descent into the sea of death.

Even if one ignores the fact that this symbolic construction is at least marginal in the Western symbolism of the resurrection, the question remains whether it can take on visible and tangible form by means of the plunging of the lighted paschal candle into the water and the prayer that the *virtus Spiritus Sancti* will come down into the baptismal font. Has not an image which may perhaps have become unpleasant but which nevertheless remained pregnant with meaning been replaced by a web of ideas that may have been theologically cleaned up but can only be realised visually with difficulty? The poetic and theological strength of the new rite of the blessing of baptismal water is to be found not in its second but in its first part, in the recalling of the paradigms involving water. Corresponding to this is a specific understanding of blessing, the logic of which no longer stretches as far as the second part in its present form. What is involved is water. God, who created water, has had a long history of dealings with this creation of his, and this history finds its completion in baptism. By going through a series of stories from the Old and New Testaments this one and everywhere identical *creatura aquae* acquires a historical weight of meaning that transcends its material qualities. While the poetic theologian who is considering baptism reads the history of water initiated and continued by the creator of the world out of the writings of the Old and New Testaments, he is praising God and creation and placing the sacrament not just within the individual history of mankind but also within the history of the material world. The blessing that arises from this *anamnesis* is an act of recognition. If God is asked here and now to bless the water, he is asked also to regard this actual quantity of water that is here before our eyes as his creation and in fact as the creation that has acquired its own individual identity and significance in the history that has just been recalled. But this blessing that honours the creature water and that is indicated in the poetic series of paradigms about water has not yet taken on an adequate liturgical form in the current version of the rite.   -

5. THE BLESSING OF WATER IN THE BAPTISMAL RITES

The formula for the blessing of baptismal water in the Easter Vigil has been taken over as the normal form for the new baptismal rites of the *Rituale Romanum* (*Ordo baptismi parvulorum* § 54: 91; *Ordo initiationis christianae adultorum* § 258), with the minor modification that the plunging of the paschal candle into the water is replaced in these cases by moving the water with the hand. The repertoire of gestures seems to be relatively arbitrary. Alongside this normal form two alternative formulations are provided for use *ad libitum* (the first, OBP § 223, OICA § 389:1; the second OBP § 224, 118, 142, OICA § 389: 2). A detailed analysis of these texts is not possible here, particularly with regard to the variations allowed in the different vernaculars. But some tendencies can be pointed out:

(*a*) The gesture of blessing which by the nature of things directs attention on to the substance of water remains cut down and relatively arbitrary (moving with the hand or the sign of the cross) and in certain cases can even be dispensed with.

(*b*) The idea of *benedictio et invocatio Dei super aquam* here comes fully to the surface, especially in the litany-like structure which provides suitable acclamations and invocations for the congregation (*Benedictus Deus*; *Exaudi nos, Domine*).

(*c*) We have to note a tendency towards systematising baptismal theology (e.g. by a trinitarian appropriation of the water paradigms) and towards making the texts of the prayers serve a didactic purpose in baptismal instruction. The semantic field of these texts is no longer focused on the subject of water itself, which is not what we find in the series of paradigms about water in the normal form.

(*d*) The blessing of the water in the narrower sense has the form of a prayer asking for a blessing (*sanctifica*, *benedic*). These prayers no longer devote any special attention to the (*creatura aquae*: water itself is only alluded to obliquely. They are really prayers for the success of the baptism that is to follow. 'Success' means here that the baptism takes place with the saving effects that have been expounded theologically and catechetically, in reality with regard to the person or persons baptised and mentally with regard to the conscious participation of those present.

In these alternative formulations the recent development of the blessing of baptismal water has moved the furthest away from the form enacted in the preconciliar Easter Vigil. This is a reason for looking back at this once again.

6. THE SHAME OF BEING A SHAMAN

Behind the reform of the rite of blessing the baptismal water we can discern the motive of severing the direct connection of the blessing with the water and the connection between the blessing and the idea of fertility. The more this is something decided on officially by Church authority, the more it is worth considering that what is being broken up here is not just a very old link in the theology and liturgy of baptism but also what from the point of view of the history of religion is the first and oldest expectation connected with blessing. In the early patriarchal stories of the Old Testament blessing has 'the primal meaning of the power of fertility and the power of thriving'.[8] 'Since blessing is something like the handing over of power, some kind of action or gesture necessarily belongs to it.'[9]

Precisely this very old link between blessing and the fruitful transmission of power was brought out in the Roman rite of the blessing of baptismal water until the reform of the liturgy. Then what had been done for centuries without any difficulty in the decent obscurity of a dead language and in the mysterious early hours of Holy Saturday was suddenly exposed to the glare of publicity. The *arcana numinis admixtio* which the celebrant enacted through words and gestures was suddenly exposed to everybody's gaze—as a magical survival. The shame was felt of being some kind of shaman in an enlightened world. So the reform did away with everything that could look like water magic, like 'charging'[10] and transforming material things. With the departure of everything that could look like the magical manipulation of the material world the Roman liturgy has in this instance adapted itself to some extent to the philosophical framework of an attitude to nature controlled by the natural sciences and technology. What is remarkable is that this should happen precisely at a time when this apparently reasonable framework of our Western civilisation should be beginning to show certain cracks and when older models of our relationship with nature and our dealings with the material world are coming to be regarded as less arrogant and even occasionally to be taken into account.

7. BLESSING AND FRUITFULNESS

The theologians of the early church had the same aversion for the fertility cults of the Hellenistic world as the prophets of Israel had for those of Canaan. But that did not stop them using the language of sexuality in their theology and liturgy of baptism. This was not of course with the aim of celebrating the mystery of human sexuality and indulging in a ritual conjuration of its fertility. Its subject was not natural birth and natural fertility but the birth of the new man or woman, the rebirth from water and the Spirit, which for them expanded to become a complex of images comprising a new conception. What was involved was the fertility of the Church, of the congregation. The fact that God's blessing could mean the fertility, growth and increase of the people of Israel is shown clearly by the traditions of the Old Testament. And at least in one passage of the New Testament (Romans 15:29) the 'blessing of Christ' would seem to consist in the Christian community growing and thriving.

What was specific to the rite of blessing the baptismal water was that this blessing was presented in the form of a ritual drama of fertilisation. In the drama of the old rite the Church reminded itself that it did not grow and increase of its own power but that the fertility, growth, increase, thriving of the community have their foundation in the creative inspiration of the Spirit and in its own openness and receptivity for this inspiration that penetrates it. Originally this rite was designed so that the new birth of baptism followed immediately on fertilisation. The conditions of the actual growth of Christian communities meant that the rite of the blessing of baptismal water could find evidence to justify its boast in baptism. But this has long been the case no more, at least in countries that have long been Christian. Communities no longer grow and increase to the extent that they can proudly display their numerous new children during the Easter Vigil and happily portray the foundation of their fecundity. Communities stagnate or shrink or are assailed by the doubt whether all the children who in keeping with custom are baptised during the year will be capable of living the new life they have been initiated into. This could perhaps be the ultimate and cruellest reason for not continuing the old rite: no longer simply civilised embarrassment or theological sensitivity about the form of representation, but doubt about the matter itself, anxiety about mocking God with a hypocritical rite.

If a Christian community today faces up to the truth, is it then so

unthinkable that it should rediscover itself in the secret lament of the childless
Hannah who poured out her soul before God (1 Sam. 1:1–18)?[11] Would the
rite in the Easter Vigil have taken on a different form if it had renewed itself
out of the abyss of a lament of this kind and had, with heart, mouth and hands,
become an urgent entreaty of God in a barren age?

Translated by Robert Nowell

Notes

1. See B. Kleinheyer 'Lobpreis und Ausrufung Gottes über dem Wasser'
Liturgisches Jahrbuch 26 (1976) 138–155.
2. E. Stommel *Studien zur Epiklese der römischen Taufwasserweihe* (Bonn 1950)
p. 35.
3. See E. Stommel 'Die Benedictio fontis in der Osternacht' *Liturgisches Jahrbuch*
7 (1957) 8–24; S. Benz 'Zur Vorgeschichte der römischen Taufwasserweihe' *Revue
bénédictine* 66 (1956) 218–255.
4. E. Stommel *Studien* p. 61.
5. E. J. Lengling 'Die Taufwasserweihe der römischen Liturgie. Vorschlag zu einer
Neuformung' in *Liturgie, Gestalt und Vollzug* ed. W. Dürig (Munich 1963)
pp. 176–251: the reference here is to p. 233.
6. E. Stommel *Studien* p. 24.
7. See *Reallexikon für Antike und Christentum* s.v. *Empfängnis* (E. Lesky and J. H.
Waszink), vol. 4 cols 1245–1255, s.v. *Embryologie* (E. Lesky and J. H. Waszink), vol. 4
cols 1228–1244.
8. C. Westermann *Der Segen in der Bibel und im Handeln der Kirche* (Munich 1968)
p. 57.
9. *Ibid.* p. 55.
10. B. Fischer 'Die Intentionen bei der Reform des Erwachsenen- und
Kindertaufritus' *Liturgisches Jahrbuch* 21 (1971), 65–75: the reference here is to p. 70.
11. On this see A. Stock 'Strukturale Analyse—am Beispiel vol 1 Sam. 1:1–2, 21'
Katechetische Blätter 101 (1976) 523–534. On the whole question, see A. Stock 'Ostern
feiern. Eine semiotische Untersuchung zur Osterliturgie' in *Ostern in Bildern, Reden,
Riten, Geschichten und Gesängen* ed. A. Stock and M. Wichelhaus (Zürich 1979)
pp. 103–128.

Gabriele Winkler

The Blessing of Water in the Oriental Liturgies

WATER IS blessed in the baptismal liturgy and at the Feast of the Epiphany. This immediately reveals an interesting connection between Christian baptism and the baptism of Jesus in the Jordan, for, as is well known, the Baptism of Jesus is celebrated in the oriental rites on 6 January in a most solemn manner. Two fundamental types can be discerned in Oriental baptismal liturgies: the oldest, Syro-Armenian strand of tradition is anchored exclusively in John 3:5. The Byzantine rite and those dependent on it, like the later development of the Syrian liturgy towards the end of the fourth and the beginning of the fifth century (for christological reasons) integrate Rom. 6 into their *rituales*, and we can clearly demonstrate the existence of that more ancient stratum which had deliberately excluded the death-mysticism of the Epistle to the Romans.

1. THE PATRISTIC TESTIMONY

First we must assume that the development of the consecration of the baptismal water occurred earlier than that of the consecration of oil—putting on one side the Acts of Thomas, which attributed the greatest significance to the oil of anointing.[1] Also, in historical perspective, baptism in a river, i.e. in *aqua viva*, must be regarded as prior to the development of the consecration of water. In Syria (and hence in Armenia too) the original custom of baptising in a river was intimately connected with the baptism of Jesus in the Jordan.[2] Particularly illuminating is the consecration of water in the Syrian acts of

53

John. We have two accounts of it.[3] The consecration is embedded in an account of a miracle,[4] which, interestingly, alludes to Gen. 1:2 and Isa. 6:3. Important perspectives have already been established here, for a well-profiled Genesis-mysticism forms the basis of the original Syrian rite, as we can see in Aphrahat: 'At the hour at which the priests summon the Spirit, he opens heaven and comes down and broods over the face of the water.'[5] In the second account in the Acts of John we discern a further element, which is of first importance for the primitive form of the Syro-Armenian type of baptism, namely, the deliberate mimesis of the Jordan event. Thus we read in the Acts of John, for instance: 'Yea, Lord, sanctify this water with thy voice which resounded over the Jordan, indicating our Lord Jesus and saying: "This is my beloved Son" . . . For thou art here just as thou wert at the Jordan . . .'[6] Besides the example of the baptism of Jesus and Gen. 1:2, John 3:5 also plays a significant part, as Theodore of Mopsuestia, for example, shows (Hom. III, 9–10): '. . . you are not baptised with ordinary water but with the water of the second birth, which does not come to pass without the descent of the Holy Spirit. Therefore it is necessary for the priest to pray to God that the grace of the Holy Spirit may come upon the water and empower it to become a womb for this birth . . .'[7] There follows an explanation of John 3. It is noteworthy that at one time the Syrian consecration of water had no exorcism, and that the invocation is built on the baptism of Jesus, John 3:5 and Gen. 1:2. Thus the pneumatic emphasis of the ritual is unmistakable.

A different view informs the blessing of water in the Apostolic Constitutions which originate in the Syro-Palestinian area. Here John 3:5 is not the core, but Rom. 6: 'Look down from heaven and sanctify this water and imbue it with grace and power, so that he who is baptised according to the commandment of Thy Christ may be crucified, may die and be buried with him, and may rise again with him to adoption . . . so that, dead to sin, he may live in righteousness.'[8]

Thus, at the end of the fourth century, we have two basic types: the Pauline, *christocentric* death-mysticism and the Johannine, *pneumatic* birth-mysticism, and, as I have demonstrated in several studies,[9] the latter is rooted in Gen. 1:2 as well as in John 3:5. The continuing development also shows that those rites which are so firmly anchored in the creation account (with its centre of gravity in Gen. 1:2), in the descent of the Spirit upon Jesus at the Jordan, and in the pneumatic birth (John 3:5), tend not to accept exorcisms into their *rituale*, unlike the Armenian order of baptism, for instance, and those rites which, by adopting the view of a dying with Jesus on the cross (Rom. 6), were thus also receptive to the repudiation of Satan in the exorcisms.

2. THE LITURGICAL FORMULAS

In the Oriental baptismal rites, particularly among the Syrians, but also among the Copts and Ethiopians, the blessing of water was gradually assimilated to the eucharistic liturgy.[10] In the case of the Syrians this process of assimilation to the *Canon Missae* was already complete before the seventh century.[11] Again, two tendencies can be observed: on the one hand the blessing of water was complemented by elements taken from the Eucharistic Prayer (e.g. with the Syrians and Copts), and on the other there were those rites in which the blessing of water was simply enriched with readings (e.g. the Armenians). This appears to have come from the solemn reading of John 3 which is common to both East Syrians and Armenians.[12] Thus the theme of rebirth by water and the Spirit is the nucleus: material from the Old and/or New Testament was subsequently added to it by analogy with the liturgy of the Mass (e.g. Ezek. 36:25–28; Gal. 3:24–29 in the case of the Armenians; 1 Cor. 10:1–13 with the East Syrians), then, in the case of the Syrians and Copts, it was expanded by a proliferation of borrowings from eucharistic formulas.[13] The following seems to have been part of the original structure of these formulas: the universalist Ps. 28 (*Syr, Armen, Copt, Ethiop*), John 3:1–8 (*E. Syr, Armen*, [*Copt, Ethiop*]), intercession (in epicletic form and/or reference to the baptism of Jesus) together with prayer (epiclesis) and the pouring of oil into the water, which once again emphasises the pneumatic character of the blessing of water.[14]

By contrast to the Greek (and Greek-influenced) formulas, the original Syro-Armenian type of blessing of water has no exorcisms. Equally unknown is the Pauline theology of baptism, which the Maronites and Armenians have never used as the foundation for the blessing of water.

(a) The Vocabulary and the Themes Used in the Invocation[15]

Brock has convincingly shown that, on an analysis of the words, two basic types exist, i.e., the epiclesis, which uses the word 'come', and forms using the word 'send'. In the Greek and West Syrian texts (and those influenced by them) we find a request for the 'sending' of the Spirit, whereas in the East Syrian and Maronite epicleses (and forms dependent upon the East Syrian, as, for instance, in the Armenian intercessions at the blessing of water) it is the 'coming' of the Spirit (or of Jesus) that is prayed for.[16] Wherever we can show the verb 'come' (imperative), we must assume it to be very ancient, whereas 'send' does not establish itself until the fifth century.[17] We must also remember that what we have is often not a prayer for the descent of the *Spirit* but an epiclesis directed to *Christ*,[18] as e.g. in the Acts of Thomas, which presents us with the most ancient form of Christ-epiclesis (not 'Logos'-epiclesis!) in the

form of a chain of imperatives: 'Come, Holy Name of the Messiah (= Christ)!
Come, Power of Grace . . .!' etc.[19] Here we sense an immediacy and receptivity
in prayer which has been extinguished in the later formulas, where the request
is addressed to the Father, that he will 'send' the Spirit, or that the Spirit 'may
come'.

The 'send . . . and sanctify' (influenced by the Greek Anaphora of
Chrysostom) and similar pairs of terms also belong to a later time.[20] Contrary
to Brock, I believe that the combined forms in which Jesus is addressed:
'May Thy . . . Spirit come, O Lord, and rest . . . upon this water',[21] are of
considerable antiquity. The same also applies, surely, to the assertion
(influenced by John 1:32) that the Spirit 'came down and rested'. Since the
archetype of Christian baptism is the baptism of Jesus, the Jordan event is
often associated with the blessing of water, as e.g. with the East Syrians:
'. . . (the Spirit) who *came down* and *remained* on our Saviour' (see John 1:32).[22]
My assumption rests primarily on the fact that in the Spirit-christology of
the High Middle Ages the 'remaining' (= Gk John 1:32) and 'resting'
(= Diatessaron Commentary + *Armen* John 1:32) of the Spirit on Jesus at the
Jordan play such a prominent part,[23] and for that reason, no doubt, were
adopted at a very early stage into the Syrian (and Armenian) baptismal
catechesis and liturgy, which, as we know, is most closely modelled on the
baptism of Jesus with its markedly pneumatic features.

Here Christ or the *Spirit of Christ* is entreated once again to re-activate the
womb of the water, just as Jesus arose out of the Jordan and began his public
life on the basis of the Spirit's 'remaining' in or 'resting' on him. Interestingly
enough, it is here that traces remain of one of the oldest conceptions of Jesus.
Thus e.g. Aphrahat (VI, 17) speaks of the *maternal Spirit* who *gave birth* to
Jesus in the Jordan: 'Observe, Beloved, that our Lord, *who was born of that
Spirit*, was not tempted by the evil one before he received the Spirit in
baptism.'[24] Now we know that the Holy Spirit as Mother was once a
widespread theologoumenon in Syria. This idea of God's Spirit as Mother can
also be demonstrated in the early Armenian sources and the Armenian
baptismal hymns (many of which are also sung at Epiphany and Pentecost!) In
the oldest Armenian history (*Agathangeli Historia*) we read of the *womb of the
maternal Spirit* of God; here the morning of creation and the birth by water
and the Spirit (John 3:5) are woven into a unity:

And just as he separated the first earth from the waters . . .
[and] by water made all animals fruitful . . .
in like manner he caused the womb of the baptismal water to bring forth,
once again opening *the womb of the invisible Spirit*
by visible water . . .[25]

Elsewhere there is an allusion to baptism 'by water and *the womb of the Spirit*'. As far as I know, this archaic approach, originating in Syria, has only survived in a few Syrian sources, as e.g. in the Maronite and West Syrian orders of baptism:

> Blessed art Thou, Lord, God, by whose ... gift this water has been hallowed through the descent of Thy Holy Spirit, so that it has become *the womb of the Spirit, bringing* the new man *to birth* out of the old.[26]

Similarly we find in a Syrian baptismal hymn: '. . . outspread your wings, Holy Church, and receive the perfect sheep, *born by the Holy Spirit* in the water of baptism . . .'[27] But the idea has also survived in the Armenian baptismal hymns:

> Today the birth-pangs of the first Mother come to an end,
> for those who were born unto death
> are *reborn by the Spirit* to be sons of light . . .
> Thou (= Holy Spirit) who art co-Creator
> like the Father and the Son,
> by whom creatures are born to life in water,
> today dost Thou *give birth* to sons of God from the water.
> Spirit of God, have mercy.
>
> Thou who didst fashion all creatures, brooding over the waters,
> now, descending into the water-basin,
> *Thou bringest sons of God to birth* . . .[28]

Here the Genesis account and the Baptism of Jesus as the pattern of Christian baptism ('Today dost Thou give birth to *sons of God* . . . descending . . . Thou bringest *sons of God* to birth') are linked together. However, the event of Pentecost is also recalled in the pouring of oil into the baptismal water,[29] for the descent of the Spirit upon the disciples is the fulfilment of the promise of baptism by fire. Accordingly, the theological axis runs through the creative power of the Spirit of God on the morning of creation, the descent of the Spirit at the baptism of Jesus, which is the source of his public life, and the event of Pentecost, whereby the disciples become apostles in the inebriation of the Spirit ('Praise in the highest to the ... Holy Spirit, by whom the apostles became drunk with the immortal chalice, and earth was invited to heaven.') No word of the Flood, or of dying with Jesus, or of the banishing of Satan and other components so familiar to the West! Of course all this reflects the most ancient stratum of baptismal theology; in no other Oriental rite has it been preserved in such purity as in the Armenian (and, in part, in the Maronite).

In principle we can say that the tremendous wealth of symbolism was drawn from the Old and New Testaments. This is particularly true of the Syrians. In connection with the anaphora, the latter speaks of the 'overshadowing' (Luke 1:35) of the water, of the 'waters of stillness' (Ps. 23:2), of the primal water (Gen. 1:2) over which the Spirit 'flutters' with his wings (see esp. the Maronites), and of the water which flowed from the side of Jesus (John 19:34). Here the connection is clearly made with the creation account: Jesus 'slept on the cross just as Adam fell into a deep sleep; his side was pierced and from it came forth the Daughter of Light', just as Eve once came forth from the side of Adam (Jacob of Sarug). Bridal mysticism, in the context of baptism, takes up this theme, since Jesus, emerging from the Jordan waters, has become the cosmic Bridegroom (see Ephrem). Thus the Acts of John salute him, newly baptised: 'Peace be with Thee, O new Bridegroom!' Bridal mysticism in baptism has been especially well preserved among the Maronites.[30]

Interestingly, water is also viewed as the oven, and the Spirit appears in the guise of its fiery heat. This may be connected with the Diatessaron, according to which a light shone at the baptism of Jesus. The baptism of Jesus has had such a profound influence on Christian baptism that, among the Syrians (and following them, the Copts) even the baptismal spring is called 'Jordan'. And, since the water is interpreted as a maternal womb, the Syrians never designate the water of baptism as a 'grave', nor is the baptisand 'buried' in it.

(b) The Exorcism

Exorcism represents a secondary development in the Syrian blessing of water. We can see this from the Armenian rite, which is closest to the Syrian baptismal liturgy, and which has no exorcisms at the blessing of water. It seems, then, that the exorcism only came into the Syrian *rituale* through Greek influence. This can be shown in the case of the Maronite blessing of water. There we read, as the water is breathed on: 'Drive all the power of the adversary from this water, from those who enter and are baptised in it, and from this place . . .!' Then the text continues in typically Syrian style: 'Grant it the power of the Holy Spirit, that this womb of baptismal water may bring to birth heavenly and incorruptible sons, in place of the womb of Eve, which gave birth to mortal and corruptible sons. . . .'[31] The brief exorcism is probably a later interpolation as a result of external influence, i.e. it was not part of the original prayer; in fact the prayer continues in a way totally at variance with the introductory exorcism. Several manuscripts even lack the reference to the water altogether! Thus we must assume that the prayer's exorcistic opening once belonged to another part of the *rituale* and not to the blessing of water.[32] Possibly the invocation once began with: 'Grant (this water) the power of the Holy Spirit . . .'

The most ancient Constantinopolitan rite of baptism has come down to us in the *Codex Barberini* 336 (eighth/ninth century). It introduces the blessing of water with a prayer of intercession, followed by the secret 'May the kind and merciful God . . .' with its ekphonesis 'Great art Thou, O Lord . . .', which goes on: '. . . Thou didst hallow the waves of the Jordan, didst send Thy Holy Spirit from heaven, and hast crushed the heads of the dragons . . . sanctify this water . . . make it a source of purity . . . a defence against sickness, the destruction of demons, whither the enemy cannot approach . . .' Thereupon the priest breathes thrice upon the water and signs it, with the following exorcism: 'Through the sign and the mark (*typos*) of the cross of Thy Christ may every power of the adversary be scattered! May all spiritual and unseen phantoms (*eidola*) vanish, and may no dark demon lurk in this water. We pray Thee, Lord, let no impure spirit descend into the water with him who is baptised . . . but, O Lord of the universe, declare this water to be the water of stillness, the water of redemption, the water of sanctification . . . that they may be implanted into the image of Thine only-begotten Son, and by baptism be made also partakers of the resurrection (Rom. 6) . . .'[33]

This proves that the Pauline theology of baptism and the use of exorcisms go hand in hand. Wherever we hear of the extinguishing of the baptisand's former life in the baptismal water, we can also expect exorcisms. On the other hand the rites which are built on the Johannine theology of baptism, including Genesis and the baptism of Jesus, attribute no significance to exorcisms. The driving out of Satan and the invocation of the Spirit (or of the Spirit of Christ) are antithetical to each other. The Pauline, *christocentric* death-mysticism and the Johannine Genesis-mysticism with its strong *pneumatic* thrust represent fundamentally different theological approaches.

Translated by Graham Harrison

Notes

1. See G. Winkler 'Das armenische Initiationsrituale' in *Orient. Chr. Analecta* (1982) 142–143, 170, 412.

2. *Ibid.* 143, 170–171.

3. See W. Wright *Apocryphal Acts of the Apostles II* (London 1871) pp. 39, 53–54; Winkler 'Initiationsrituale' 147–148, 152–153.

4. There must be a general connection here between the reference to light and fire and the Diatessaron, since, as is well known, the latter speaks of a light shining at the baptism of Jesus.

5. D. A. Parisot 'Aphraatis Sapientis Persae Demonstrationes' in *Patrol. Syr. I* (Paris 1894) pp. 291ff; Winkler 'Initiationsrituale' 162–163.

6. See Wright *Apocryphal Acts* pp. 53–54.

7. See H. M. Riley 'Christian Initiation' in *Studies in Chr. Antiquity 17* (Washington 1974) pp. 332–338.

8. Lib. VII, 43, 5; F. X. Funk *Didascalia et Constitutiones Apostolorum* (Paderborn 1905) p. 450.

9. Listed in the index of Winkler 'Initiationsrituale' at p. 471 under 'Tauftheologie'.

10. This development was not followed by the Byzantine Rite: cf. F. C. Conybeare *Rituale Armenorum* (Oxford 1905) pp. 399ff; J. Goar *Euchologion* (Venice ²1730) pp. 287ff.

11. See S. Brock 'Studies in the Early History of the Syrian Orthodox Baptismal Liturgy' in *Journal of Theol. Studies 23* (1972) 40–44.

12. See *The Liturgy of the Holy Apostles . . . and . . . Baptism* (London 1893) p. 71: John 2:23–3:8, whereas the Copts and Ethiopians place John 3:1–21 directly prior to the blessing of water; see H. Denzinger *Ritus Orientalium* (Würzburg 1863) pp. 201, 225, and the West Syrian Rite and the Maronites read John 3 at the Rite of the Catechumenate, which is possibly a secondary development; see J. A. Assemani *Codex Liturgicus I* (Rome 1749) p. 229; A. Mouhanna 'Les Rites de l'initiation dans l'Église maronite' in *Or.Chr. Anal. 212* (Rome 1980) 153, 162, 175, 178.

13. See Mouhanna 'L'Initiation' 66, 93, 108, 119 *passim*; Brock 'Early History' 41; Assemani II, pp. 162–176; Denzinger pp. 219, 230.

14. See Winkler 'Initiationsrituale' 423–432, 445–446; on the Coptic and Ethiopian Rites cf. Denzinger pp. 219, 230.

15. Cf. Brock 'Early History'; *id.*, 'The Epiklesis in the Antiochean Baptismal Ordines' in *Orient. Chr. Analecta 197* (Rome 1974) 183–218; *id.*, *The Holy Spirit in the Syrian Baptismal Tradition* (The Syrian Church Ser. 9) (Poona 1979) pp. 70–115; *id.*, 'The Consecration of the Water in the Oldest Mss. of the Syr. Orthod. Bapt. Liturgy' in *Orient Chr. Periodica 37* (1971) 317–332.

16. See Brock 'Epiklesis' 199–200, 213–215; *id.*, *Holy Spirit* p. 70; Winkler 'Initiationsrituale' 429.

17. See Brock 'Epiklesis' 213–214.

18. *Ibid.*, 188–189, 197–198, 213. The Christ-epiclesis has also been preserved in the Maronites and Armenians; see Mouhanna 'L'Initiation' 220; Winkler 'Initiationsrituale' 427–429, 446.

19. *N.b.* these concern the pre-baptismal anointing; see Brock 'Epiklesis' 213; Winkler 'Initiationsrituale' 138.

20. See Brock 'Epiklesis' 214.

21. See details of texts in Brock 'Epiklesis 190; *id.*, 'Holy Spirit' 71.

22. See details of texts in Brock 'Epiklesis 189; *id.*, *Holy Spirit* p. 71.

23. See G. Winkler 'Ein bedeutsamer Zusammenhang . . .' in *Le Muséon 96* (1983) 267–326.

24. *Ibid.* 322.

25. *Ibid.* 323; *eadem* 'Die Taufhymnen der Armenier' in H. Becker and R. Kaczinski *Liturgie und Dichtung I* (St Ottilien 1983) pp. 394, 396.

26. Quoted in Brock *Holy Spirit* p. 84; Winkler 'Taufhymnen' p. 397.

27. Quoted in Brock *Holy Spirit* p. 4; Winkler 'Taufhymnen' p. 397.

28. See Winkler 'Taufhymnen' pp. 386–388, 394.

29. Source material in Winkler 'Taufhymnen' p. 387.

30. See Mouhanna 'L'Initiation' 33, 38, 73, 88, 125 *passim*.

31. *Ibid.*, p. 53.

32. *Ibid.*, p. 82. (Mouhanna failed to draw any conclusions from this important discovery).

33. See Conybeare *Rituale Armenorum* pp. 397–401; Goar pp. 287–289.

Laurent Mpongo

Contemporary African Celebration of the Blessing of the Baptismal Water in the Roman Rite

IN 1956, Black priests from all over the world ventured to explore the relation between Christianity and negritude.[1] In the world of those days there were a few well-disposed people who sympathised with them, but in many areas there were considerable reservations. It is true that in 1956 the Black priests were talking in terms of adaptations. Much water has flowed under the bridge since then, and today we can speak freely of the dialogue between the faith and different cultures. More than that, it is accepted as normal that each people should express the faith through its own culture. It is therefore no longer a question of adaptation but of 'inculturation', to use a term which is now gaining currency.

This is the context in which I, as a Black priest, would like to discuss the way in which the blessing of the baptismal water in the revised Roman liturgy is practised in the Catholic communities of Black Africa. I shall begin by recalling the symbolism of the baptismal water in the Roman liturgy. Then I shall explain the symbolism of water in Black Africa, and discuss the relation between belief, symbol and human behaviour. In this way the reader may come to understand how much has yet to be done in Christian Africa in order that the blessing of the baptismal water may be done in accordance with an 'incultured' Christian liturgy.

1. BAPTISMAL WATER IN THE REVISED ROMAN LITURGY

The Christian communities of Black Africa bless the baptismal water on Easter Eve and on the occasion of adult and infant baptisms, in accordance with the regulations of the Roman Missal and the baptismal rituals promulgated by Paul VI. I am dealing here with the formula common to these liturgical books.[2]

Let it be said straight away that this formula refers in the first place to the waters at the beginning of the creation of the world. Water seemed to be endowed with a sanctifying divine power. The formula also recalls the baptismal symbolism of the waters of the Flood, and of the crossing of the Red Sea. It goes on to mention the baptism of Jesus in the Jordan, the mystery of the water and blood which flowed from the side of Christ as he hung on the cross, and the command given by Jesus to his disciples to go and teach and baptise all nations. After these references, there is a prayer that God will make the water the means whereby men are cleansed from every stain and begotten to a new life.

During the Easter Vigil, the priest plunges the Easter candle into the water once or three times, as he thinks fit. But when he is celebrating baptism on an occasion other than Easter Eve, the priest touches the water with his right hand. In both cases, as he performs the action he calls upon the Spirit of God to take possession of the water. Finally, as he performs one or other of these actions, the priest declares that the baptismal water is the means by which men share in the mystery of the death and resurrection of Christ. The congregation say 'Amen' in response, and the priest withdraws his hand, or the Paschal candle, from the water.

In Black Africa the Christian liturgy will give fuller expression to the rich symbolism of water. To this end, it must show why water possessed by the Spirit of God has power to make a man into a new creature. It will tell how the water is at one and the same time a symbol of God, the source of all life, and a symbol of the Holy Spirit.[3] The Christian liturgy will explain that the Holy Spirit is God's supreme gift, made available to men by virtue of the mystery of the incarnation and glorification of Christ. The baptismal water must be seen to be the medium in which men receive the life of God, and share in the lot of Christ himself, crucified and risen. Also, as Black Africans see it, water possessed by divine power is an agent of cleansing and of healing. Consequently Christian symbolism of the baptismal water has to take account of African water-symbolism in general and of lustral water in particular.

2. THE SYMBOLISM OF WATER IN BLACK AFRICA

Black African traditions know nothing of the use of baptismal water as such. They use only rain-water, or the water of springs, rivers, or wells,[4] not forgetting, of course, the lustral use of water.

I would like to discuss now the symbolism of water in general and that of lustral water in particular. The creation myths of many ethnic groups in Black Africa[5] depict water as a force which, from the beginning, has always been under the control and direction of a spirit. In some settings, the spirit has male characteristics. In others, it appears as female. In neither case is the spirit, which kept the water under control by containing it within receptacles or a great calabash, identified with the hero-creator of the world. In all the myths, the hero-creator took control of the water by paralysing or killing the spirit which had possessed it from the beginning. But this action produced problems, in that he had no sooner disarmed his adversary than the water-receptacles themselves burst apart. The water flowed from them in a raging torrent, and spread everywhere, destroying everything in its path. Water is thus the symbol of death. At the same time, wherever it rested water was endowed with a procreative capacity.

As I have already said, the spirit which possessed the water could be regarded as either male or female, depending upon the particular tradition. Consequently it is not surprising that the water should have been thought of as containing masculine or feminine seeds of life, put there by the guardian spirit of the waters. It is surely this action of the spirit in fertilising the water that is repeated today when the practitioners add certain ingredients to the water in order to strengthen its procreative power.[6]

Rich with these seeds of life, the water is thought of as a mother. Not only does it cause life to spring from the earth into which it goes, but it also makes fertile every woman in whose body it is collected, as in a calabash. This mother-water is called living water, because it gives to every being permeated by it the power which it has itself received from the fertilising spirit. Anyone who is ill will be washed in water in order to be purified. In Black Africa, water purifies because it is the medium through which the hero-creator takes possession of every human creature and transforms his wretchedness into happiness and his infirmities into health. In a word, water is a purifying agent or an agent of healing. In fact water is the weapon used by the hero-creator to combat every power which harms man or makes his environment hostile.

Consequently, to be purified by water means to be saved. It is to recover one's vital force, and to live in an environment which encourages one's rest and growth. So, in Black Africa, water which is to purify a person must necessarily be sprinkled towards the four cardinal points so as to free them from bondage to any power hostile to men. In the light of this symbolism of water, it is easier to understand the importance of lustral water in the life of Black Africans.

As is well known, water is regarded as a polyvalent beneficial symbol.[7] It symbolises goodness, purity, good fortune, strength. In addition, because of its natural properties, it has other symbolical meanings. Cold, or fresh, water is a symbol of health, and gives growth. This is the case with rain, spring, or river water. Conversely, warm or tepid water is a symbol of disease, which is thought of as hot, like fever. It must be said that Black Africans try to strengthen the power of water. To achieve this, their practitioners are accustomed to add certain ingredients to the water. In particular, so far as water with which it is intended to bless people or their environment is concerned, the most frequently used ingredient is kaolin. Some ethnic groups make a similar use of red ochre.

Kaolin is regarded as a medicine. It has power to make a person strong or to give him success in whatever he undertakes. With many ethnic groups, kaolin is even a symbol for the sperm, which esoteric language calls blood purified by water.

Depending on the circumstances, red ochre can symbolise misfortune, physical weakness, or lack of success in what one undertakes. When it symbolises physical weakness, red ochre refers to menstrual blood.[8]

Mixed with kaolin, water is a symbol of life and good fortune. Among the Ndembu people of Zambia, for example, water mixed with kaolin and red ochre, and sprinkled on a patient, signifies a blessing or the conjugal act, as the case may be.[9]

All things considered, water used for the blessing of individuals and their surroundings is seen as a charm bringing success. All the evidence suggests that this symbolism of water is to be understood in the light of the relations which exist between religious belief, the symbol which represents it, and the human behaviour by which it is expressed in society.

3. RELIGIOUS BELIEF, SYMBOLS AND HUMAN BEHAVIOUR

Black Africans do not find it easy to make a distinction between religious belief (doctrine), the symbols which represent it and serve to locate it in time and space, and the human behaviour by which it is expressed within human communities. These three realities all hang together. When they are separated within the life of an individual they become uncertain.

Religious belief (doctrine) is the expression of the relationship which exists between man, his environment and the supernatural. As such, religious belief tells a man what he should do, not only to maintain his relationship with his fellow-man and with his family or clan, but also to live out his relationship with the supernatural and with his environment. Black Africans believe strongly that a person grows, develops his vital force and makes a success of life by living out this complex network of relationships. At the same time, religious ritual is regarded as the means by which religious belief becomes part of life, and finds, in the behaviour of the believer, a suitable form of establishing itself in time and space, and of being transmitted, unambiguously, to succeeding generations. In order to bring his religious belief right into his own life and into the life of the human group to which he belongs, the believer will have recourse to symbols. These symbols may be objects, natural phenomena, or words—passwords or counter-signs. He will make use of these because, in his eyes, they are the realities which permit him to enter into communion with the supernatural, with his environment and with his fellow-men.[10] By doing this, the believer will feel himself to be supported by the supernatural, by his fellows and by his environment. This alone makes his survival possible. All religious belief, therefore, leads to action. It causes the believer to employ symbols in order to make tangible his relationship with the supernatural, his fellows and an environment which he has to try to make more habitable. In this way, religious belief is embodied in a form of human behaviour commonly called ritual action. In the last resort, religious ritual is neither more nor less than the kind of behaviour a believer adopts in order to live out his relationship with the supernatural, his fellows and an environment which he is trying to humanise. In the course of time, this behaviour falls into a fixed, stereotyped form. The believer will employ religious symbols, will say identical forms of words, and will repeat the same actions and formulas in similar situations, in order to demonstrate the way in which he understands, lives out, expresses, professes and bears witness to his relationship with the supernatural, his fellows and his environment. The believer is not neglecting his social obligations when he devotes time to this network of relationships. It is rather the way by which he seeks to satisfy his felt needs.

This is not the place to investigate the function of religious ritual[11] in the sense referred to above. Nevertheless we may suppose that human behaviour based on religious belief, which is clear and explicit because it is well represented by an appropriate symbol, is one of the factors responsible for the changes which take place at the heart of human society. Such behaviour strengthens the cohesion of the human group by arousing in believers the desire to organise themselves and co-operate in devising and carrying out activities which make the environment more human, and more conducive to the expansion and development of human life. Moreover, by adopting the same patterns of behaviour in society, believers succeed in uncovering those elements which sustain that society and give them their identity: a common religious belief, identical religious values to preserve, the same needs to satisfy. Finally, that form of human behaviour which, thanks to the use of religious symbols, establishes man's relationship to the supernatural, to his fellows and to his environment, is, without a doubt, the area in which the believer responds to the unceasing call to protect himself against all the forces which are threatening him. It is also the area in which the believer is constantly invited to entrust himself to the supernatural, and to persist in hope.

This, it seems to me, is the context in which, in a Black African setting, we should consider the blessing of the baptismal water. Black Africans will respond to the water of baptism with greater joy and enthusiasm than they do today, as they come to understand it as a symbol representing faith expressed in a form of human activity in society, which has as its object that man's environment should not be hostile to him.

4. PROSPECTS FOR THE FUTURE

The unity which exists between religious belief, the symbol which makes belief visible, and the human behaviour which bears witness to it before other people, demands that theological thought in Black Africa should cease to be mere speculation, using language which does not lead to action. This necessity becomes all the more pressing because at the present time the Catholic Church is resolved to define more clearly the relations which exist between faith and different cultures.

It is true that the Pontifical Council for Culture has not yet spoken the last word on the subject. Nevertheless, relations between faith and different cultures require that every possible effort should be made to ensure that Christian communities in Black Africa, and everywhere else in the world where Blacks live, cease to be deprived of their structure through the tendency towards a life-style which separates faith, symbol and human behaviour. In particular, when they perform the ceremony of the baptismal water, Christian communities in the Black world ought first and foremost to recognise that there is a correlation between belief, symbol and human behaviour.

This is not an attempt to go back to a separation of sacred and secular at the very moment when the liturgy we have inherited from the West is moving in the opposite direction. Rather it is the affirmation of a conviction: that culture is not simply something to be christianised, but is essentially the instrument God uses to touch the spirit and the heart of men, so that they may plan and organise their life and their environment in the light of the love of God, which inspires them from the moment when they become the temple of the Holy Spirit. Furthermore, the Holy Spirit not only dwells in people, but is also present in the universe. The universe owes its cohesion to the Holy Spirit, who unites the world and gives a voice to every created thing,[12] so that it may confess God's glory.[13] Man is himself a part of this universe filled with the Spirit of God, and it is therefore natural that the universe should be the starting-point for man's attempt to affirm and live out his relationship with God and his fellows. If the Christian liturgy claims to be cosmic in its scope, it is obviously right that the worship offered by man to God should be defined as 'the religious man's tendency to express his relations with the invisible world by taking the elements of culture and of creation as his point of departure'.[14]

I have already mentioned the way in which the new Roman liturgical books bring faith to life by means of the symbolism of the water of baptism.[15] I have also made suggestions as to how this faith may be made more explicit, so that the symbolism may become even more expressive.[16] At the same time we must hope that the liturgical action will declare that the new life received at baptism should grow and develop in a harmonious manner. There is need, therefore, for an invocation which asks that God will be the Providence constantly watching over the believer and preserving him from all evil. So God must be the guarantor of all the blessings which the Christian community invokes upon anyone who is touched by the water of baptism. Moreover, the actual text of the blessing of the baptismal water should be formulated in such a way as to make clear the relation between baptismal faith, the water which symbolises it, and the behaviour by which it is expressed in human society. Since the economy of salvation celebrated in baptism concerns the whole man, the formula for the blessing of the baptismal water should urge the one who is to be baptised, as well as the whole Christian congregation, to lead a good life in the world, and to think of things that may be done in the economic and social spheres to promote a way of life worthy of a human person, made in the image of God as revealed in his Son, a temple of the Holy Spirit. In this context, are we not going astray if our Christian liturgies fail to meet the person as he is in the world to which he belongs? Should we not ask the radical question as to whether Christian liturgies celebrated in the Black world are sufficiently integrated into the appropriate culture to enable them to fulfil the social functions required of all religions? However that may be, the Black world, tormented today by the problem of hunger, by poverty and every kind of social injustice, needs Christian liturgies integrated into its cultures, so that it may be motivated to action which will make this world a foreshadowing of the world which is to come.

CONCLUSION

The ceremony of the baptismal water is an action which affects the life of every Christian. For this reason it is right that Christians should recognise its significance. The Black world in particular would like the ceremony to become more expressive, more significant. To achieve this, the Christian liturgy should incorporate insights from African water-symbolism, while underlining the relations which exist between baptismal faith, the religious symbol which represents it, and the human behaviour by which it is expressed in society. That is the *sine qua non* by which the Christian liturgy may become the place where the Christian community recognises its role as an agent of social change, so that this present world may be a foreshadowing of the world to come.

Translated by G. W. S. Knowles

Notes

1. See *Des Prêtres noirs s'interrogent* (Paris 1956).

2. See *Missale Romanum* (Editio typica, Typis Polyglottis Vaticanis 1970) pp. 280–285; *Rituale Romanum, Ordo initiationis christianae adultorum* (Editio typica, Typis Polyglottis Vaticanis 1972) nn. 213–215; *Rituale Romanum, Ordo baptismi parvulorum* (Editio typica altera, Typis Polyglottis Vaticanis 1973) nn. 53–54.

3. See John 7:37–39. J. Daniélou *Les Symboles chrétiens primitifs* (Paris 1961) p. 49.

4. See A. B. Kiambi Yavanga *Symbolisme de l'eau dans les rites Kongo et dans la liturgie chrétienne* (Rome 1979) (unpublished).

5. See P. A. Janssens 'Het ontstaan der dingen in de Folklore der Bantus' in *Anthropos* 21 (1926) 546–565. H. Baumann *Schöpfung und Urzeit des Menschen* (Berlin² 1964).

6. See below.

7. See V. Turner *The Ritual Process* (Cornell 1979) p. 66.

8. Cf. L. V. Thomas and R. Luneau *La terre africaine et ses religions* (Paris 1980) pp. 114–115. V. Turner, the work cited in note 7, at pp. 53, 69.

9. See V. Turner, the work cited in note 7, at p. 69.

10. See A. de Waal Malefijt *Religion and Culture* (New York 1968) pp. 87, 189. F. Plog and D. G. Bates *Cultural Anthropology* (New York² 1980) p. 370.

11. See F. Plog and D. G. Bates, the work cited in note 10, at pp. 374–381.

12. See Wisdom 1:7.

13. See Psalm 19 (18):2.

14. L. Mpongo 'La Liturgie de demain au Zaïre' in *Aspects du Catholicisme au Zaïre* (Kinshasa 1981) p. 90.

15. See above.

16. See above.

PART III

Special Questions

Janet Walton

Ecclesiastical and Feminist Blessing: Women as Objects and Subjects of the Power of Blessing

THROUGHOUT LITURGICAL history women have received blessings—virgins, mothers, daughters, wives, and abbesses—but they have not had the authority to impart blessings or to propose appropriate texts for them. Feminists are raising significant questions about this situation. They are addressing the form, content, and meaning of blessings for women in current liturgical use. They are also suggesting alternative expressions of blessing for and by women. This article is an occasion to probe these questions and to establish principles which may evoke further discussion.

The material is organised in three sections:

1. An examination of two rites of blessing for women (an abbess and a mother) seen in relationship to similar blessings for men (an abbot and a father).

2. An exposition of four principles to provide a basis for an alternative, feminist rite of blessing.

3. A description, by way of example, to illustrate new possibilities of blessing which women may give and receive.

1. THE BLESSING OF AN ABBESS[1] AND OF A MOTHER[2]

The blessings designed for these two classifications of persons, from very different lifestyles, are examples of a number of blessings in current liturgical use that demonstrate a monolithic and disturbing perception of women. The demeaning nature of this perception becomes clearer when compared with similar blessings for their male counterparts. In the rite of blessing, the abbess, like the abbot, is first of all instructed. She is reminded to be obedient to the Church and the Pope, to teach her sisters by constant dedication to the monastic life and by her good example. However, unlike the abbot, she is not asked to stand in the place of Christ, to guide others in the way of the Spirit, to teach by sound doctrine, to be concerned for the spiritual good of those entrusted to her care, to be a faithful steward of goods, a good shepherd, or to pray without ceasing for God's people.

One need not wonder why a woman with very similar responsibilities to her male counterpart is not recognised fully and openly for her contributions. Clearly, female persons cannot transmit nor witness the most cherished aspects of the Christian tradition. Not only are they limited by the institutional arguments against the ordination of women and therefore cannot 'stand in the place of Christ', but, in addition, they are not acknowledged as spiritual directors, nor as teachers of the Church's doctrine. They are not identified as responsible leaders of their respective communities nor as astute collaborators in caring for the earth's resources. They are not perceived as those whose life of prayer contributes to the 'shepherding' and care of God's people. In contrast to abbots, who are given authority equal to that of a bishop, abbesses are granted minimal power.

The differences do not end here. In the final prayer of blessing in each rite, there are some significant variances in the texts. The Church petitions God to 'strengthen' the new abbot, but, to 'sustain' the new abbess. It recognises the abbot's duties as 'demanding' and 'heavy'. It does not characterise the duties of the abbess. In the prayer for the abbot, God is asked to give him 'a heart full of compassion, wisdom, and zeal so that he may not lose even one of the flock entrusted to his charge'. There is no similar section in the blessing of an abbess.

The definitions of 'strengthen' and 'sustain' offer a clue to some conclusions. To strengthen is to make powerful or strong. To sustain is to keep in existence, to maintain, prolong, provide for, or support. The respective descriptions and mandates for leadership of an abbot and abbess are based on stereotypical sex role differences rather than upon one's faithfulness in responding to God's gifts. Abbots need strength to empower, whereas abbesses need sustenance to endure. Imparting power is signified as a singular manner of participating in the work of God, 'demanding and heavy', and therefore calls for a specially endowed person. Supporting or maintaining is viewed as secondary. It does not warrant the same gifts of God.

This exposition of texts leads to a variety of conclusions:

(a) Whereas abbots and abbesses at one time were recognised as equally significant leaders in the life of a monastic community these texts show the erosion of their similar identities.

(b) Whereas God created all of humankind in God's own image, female and male (Gen. 1:27), the power to reveal God and to impart the divine tradition falls only to the male, or at least, is his in far greater proportion.

(c) Whereas both women and men are recognised by the Church as leaders of a community, the potential of that leadership is determined by gender. The potential of women is strictly limited.

These conclusions are alarming and distressing. They demand the attention of the whole Church. Should one argue that the blessing of an abbot or abbess is rarely experienced by most people, the very fact that such a rite has been published in an edition of the *Rites of the Catholic Church* as revised by the Second Vatican Council and as recently as 1980 should be a source of concern for all the Church's members. As an authorised statement, it represents the Church's perspective, one that identifies how God is known and experienced. And this statement both restricts and undermines the contributions of women.

An examination of the brief blessing for a mother and a father raises similar concerns:

Holy God,
you compare your own love
for your people
to the love of a mother
for her children.
Look with kindness
on these mothers,
give them comfort
in moments of sorrow,
and joy in their work
for their families.
Listen to their prayers,
and bless them
in all they do for you.
Let them share with
Jesus your Son
and Mary our mother
in the everlasting happiness
of Heaven.
Father, we ask this grace
through Christ our Lord.
Amen.

Lord Jesus our brother
we praise you for
    saving us.
Teach us to love you
and your Father
by keeping your
    commandments.
Bless these fathers,
and deepen their love for
    their wives and families.
By their work and example
    and prayer, may
    they lead their
    children to follow you.
Lord Jesus,
    hear our prayer as
    we offer you glory
    for ever and ever.
Amen.

The image of a mother conveyed in this blessing straddles being like God on the one hand—a person who is aware, active, and faithful—and, on the other, being helpless and weak, one whose primary responsibilities are so vague they can only be described as 'work for their families'. The representation is clearer again in contrast. The image of father is carefully defined. He is reminded that love is not ambiguous but is located in one's response to the commandments. He is acknowledged as responsible for the love among members of his family. He is commissioned to lead his children through work, example, and prayer. In both the opening and closing phrases he is recognised for his ability to offer praise and glory to God.

Both the words and the quality of the blessing offer points for our consideration. In the text for the mother the first sentence leads quite naturally to a description of God's love for her/his children which the mother actualises. 'You compare your own love . . . to the love of a mother. . . .' Instead, the quality changes, spelling out the mother's need for comfort and joy rather than enumerating her gifts or responsibilities. She is blessed simply 'for *all* she does', with no mention of anything in particular.

On the other hand, the blessing of the father is specific. Once again, like the abbot, the male person is entrusted with teaching, and an example of love, work, action, and prayer. The father is the model of the Christian tradition and is responsible for imparting it. The stereotypes perdure. The female assumes a passive role, the male an active one. The female, an inferior one, the male a superior one. The female is invisible, supportive to the male.

The very rite of blessing raises a number of questions:

(i) Do we as a Church continue to believe that men can image God more specifically than women because of the form and functions of their bodies?

(ii) Are we as a church *afraid* to accept women's experiences as interpretations of the Christian life?

(iii) Are we as a Church perpetuating an identity of men that is based on an invisible or inferior position of women and then blessing that identity?

2. A FEMINIST PERSPECTIVE

The rites for an abbess and for a mother illustrate an image of woman that is affirmed throughout the liturgical practice of the Roman Catholic Church. From within this Church, women and men are calling for repentance and change. Their call, rooted in a feminist perspective, can be expressed in concrete principles. Four of these convictions are appropriate to this topic:

(*a*) Authority is a gift, the power to impart and to receive freedom.

(*b*) 'Power is experienced as power of presence to ourselves and to each other.'[3]

(*c*) Power is shared not bestowed.

(*d*) 'Power is where power is perceived.'[4]

(a) Authority is a Gift, the Power to Convey and to Receive Freedom

To participate in the act of giving or receiving a blessing is to share in the authority of God. It is to join in the flow of power that moves between God and humankind in mysterious and unpredictable ways. It is to experience moments of freedom for oneself and others. It is to enter into a sacred arena where choice is available to everyone. It is to acknowledge what is good, beautiful, and just.

Feminists perceive blessing very differently from the traditional ideas conveyed by current ecclesiastical formulas and practice. To bless is to identify the unique dignity of every human person. To bless is to proclaim publicly that a person is released from her/his own bondage and the enslavement of society. To bless is to open new doors for self-determination.

To receive a blessing means to acknowledge the possibility of transformation for one's self and for society. To receive a blessing means to respond positively to untested experience. To receive a blessing means to give up what is known for what is yet unexplored. Rather than a static reinforcement of stereotypical images, blessing, from a feminist perspective, is an act of freeing and of being freed.

(b) 'Power is Experienced as a Power of Presence to Ourselves and to Each Other'

The long struggle of women to free themselves from imprisoning dominance, stereotypical imaging and patriarchal structures has provided a fresh understanding of power. They acknowledge power in themselves, rather than solely and primarily beyond themselves. They connect this awareness with a similar awakening in others. Personal and political power are interactive. Such a recognition affects the experience and meaning of blessing. Blessing is perceived as a form in which human beings link with the divine reality. Power from within touches the power of God and this experience is extended to another. Alice Koller describes such an encounter, 'When she blessed me, I understood that she was giving me something of what constituted the core of her being.'[5] Such a blessing is not mechanical and impersonal. It is rooted in a recognition of the locus of power. The exchange testifies to the responsibility of each individual to identify her/his power and to spread its benefits.

(c) Power is Shared not Bestowed

The most persuasive intrusion into the integrity of women has been accomplished through domination. Such superiority sets male against female as well as rich against poor, white against other races. Within a liturgical structure domination is constantly being expressed in the division of clergy and laity as well as in the exclusive use of male language for God and humankind. Females and female characteristics are rarely regarded with respect. Feminists have unmasked the evil of this situation and have identified the possession of power as a primary target. Since the rite of blessing is expression of power, it too must undergo radical changes.

Seen from a feminist perspective, blessing is a collaborative experience. Blessing is given and received simultaneously. Human beings share blessings. They give shape to that which is invisible. Such an understanding changes the content and meaning of the blessing, and it affects the form in which it is given. No longer is a situation tolerable in which some persons stand above, while others kneel or stand below with bowed heads. Blessing does not flow from high to low. It loses its authenticity when the leader uses a second person pronoun (you) instead of an inclusive one (May God bless *us*)—as though that person had no need of the grace she/he is invoking—or when one assumes a subservient position to receive a blessing. Blessings are symbols of *common* need, each for each other, as well as the divine and human. Words and gestures reinforce this concept.

(d) 'Power is Where Power is Perceived'

The overload of the tradition of centuries locates power in those individuals who are most articulate, well-educated, persuasive and authorised. The time is fast fading when a woman who walks into the parish house is satisfied to brush past a priest in the hall and to receive a requested blessing for an object or for herself. In the past she acknowledged that power, and in her view, it was transmitted.

Feminists offer an alternative view. The power to bless and be blessed is released at birth, and for Christians it is reinforced in baptism. Feminists believe what Abraham Heschel says so well, just to be is holy. All human beings can be subjects as well as receivers of blessing. Such a recognition changes one's perception of oneself as well as of others. The power to bless and receive blessing is not restricted to a few but rather abundantly available to all who are willing to accept such a privilege and responsibility.

3. A NEW MODEL OF BLESSING

Since the form, content, and meaning of blessing for and by women will be affected by the principles mentioned above, the action must be participatory both in word and gesture. Its content must emphasise women's strength, courage, and faithfulness. Its meaning must convey an image of woman whose love embraces and extends a vision of freedom. The following example shows how such a new form of blessing might be imparted and written.

The women gather in a circle. The shape of the space emphasises the collaborative power of blessing and is quite unlike the familiar hierarchical arrangement where one person faces all the others. The women connect with each other by touching through the palms of their hands. Since our hands enable us to love, play, and work, the gesture not only calls to mind the importance of this part of our body but also the interdependence of these aspects of our lives. It also makes one more aware of the warmth, power and uniqueness of the persons whom one touches. One *feels* the energy that links them. There is a moment of silence when each person can experience the power of this gesture. The words of the blessing punctuate the silence. Five women, spaced throughout the circle, read the invocation to which all respond.

Leader: Let us affirm the goodness in each other, the integrity and beauty of our bodies, the insights of our minds.
All: We stand together.
Let us acknowledge the pain in each other, the strain of struggle, the sorrow of defeat and death.
All: We stand together.
Let us uphold the daring in each other: the boldness of spirit, the resoluteness of action.
All: We stand together.
Let us esteem laughter and joy in each other: the irony of circumstances, the delight of relationships.
All: We stand together.
Let us go forth empowered from this space and time knowing that as we bless each other so we are blessed in God and with God and by God.
All: We stand together.

We, the Church, shape our liturgical history. We learn from the past in order to change the present and the future. The rite of blessing for women in present liturgical books and actions in parishes reinforces a submissive and demeaning vision of women. We, the Church, have the duty to acknowledge this misinterpretation and to initiate change. We, the Church, call each other to create a community where the rite of blessing is a symbol of our transformation.

Then women and men will feel and share more fully the unremitting love that connects them to a divine reality and to each other.

Then women and men will surrender restricted stereotypes that limit choice and freedom.

Then women and men will identify their own power and acknowledge its interdependent nature.

This invitation is the gift of women to the Church.

Notes

1. *The Rites of the Catholic Church* vol. 2 (Pueblo 1980) pp. 117–121, 127–129.
2. Canadian Conference of Catholic Bishops *A Book of Blessings* (Ottawa 1981) pp. 51–52.
3. Mary Daly 'The Qualitative Leap Beyond Patriarchal Religion' *Quest* vol. 1, no. 1, p. 21.
4. A concept credited to Delyte Frost found in Barbara Starrett 'The Metaphors of Power' in *The Politics of Women's Spirituality* edited by Charlene Spretnak (New York 1982) p. 191.
5. Alice Koller *An Unknown Woman* (New York 1983) p. 220.

Françoise Dolto (interviewed by Jacques Pohier)

The Power of Blessing over Psychic Identity

1. CURSE AND BLESSING

JACQUES POHIER: The popularization of psychology and psychoanalysis has acquainted everyone in some way with the basic function of the parents' words and gestures in forming a child's personality and identity. Do you think that blessings (or curses) can have a similar effect?

Françoise Dolto: L. Chertok, a French psychiatrist and psychoanalyst who uses suggestion treatment under hypnosis, told me that the only thing that hypnosis cannot surmount is a curse. He never succeeded in using it for that purpose. It is absolutely impossible to cancel the effects of a curse pronounced at birth. This has so profound an effect that there is no hypnosis, however deep, that can remove the curse. That I found extraordinary. A curse which a child only knows of through its parents, which is placed on the father of the child and his descendants, or on the child itself, affects the child's personality and existence, including the fruits of its labour and sexuality, throughout its life. To some extent, the same is true of a blessing. Even if it offers nothing directly, for a child a blessing is a guarantee of safety in times of difficulty, and a foothold for hope during trials and troubles. A blessing profoundly affects the symbolic order of the individual human being; hence it is irremovable. It is not supplementary to a person, like some piece of clothing. Instead it is co-existential with the human subject; and this also means co-existential with his or her creation and procreation, and therefore with the procreation of all descendants and with everything which may be called his or her issue.

Pohier: You believe, then, that blessings or curses of this kind are more powerful than the parents' wishes or words which one has to deal with in psychoanalysis. Would you say that in analysis it is possible to re-organise the effects of the parents' wishes and words?

Dolto: Yes, they can be re-organised. Remember the commandment, 'Honour thy father and thy mother . . .' (notice, it does not say: 'Love them' but 'Honour them'). As we know, 'honouring one's father and mother' sometimes involves ignoring what they told us. When they are small, children think they are loving when they are obedient. When they grow older, they realise that some instances of obedience have a pernicious influence in life thereafter, because they possess a retrograde and archaic aspect which keeps them as their parents' 'little boy' or 'little girl', maintaining their fears of the risks of life. Some people can and should think it is possible to reject all that precisely in order to honour the life which their traumatised and neurotic parents gave them. But it is impossible to ignore what was said when someone uttered a curse. Indeed, someone who has pronounced a curse marks the unconscious ineradicably. Why? Why does a curse impose a narcissistic wound which is apparently irreversible and ineradicable? Perhaps the person who utters the curse is overvalued by the relevant parental or social reference group? Perhaps it is because, when he or she utters a curse, the person in question appeals to a power of conviction which surpasses any human instance: to God, in other words? Surely a curse—as far as the person who utters it is concerned—always refers, ultimately, to God.

Pohier: Does this reference to God constitute the difference between the effect of blessings and curses and the effect of parental desires, words and gestures?

Dolto: Those wishes, words and gestures comprise a kind of unconscious guidance for the child; ultimately they are a form of gestural, ideational or verbal language: a psychic communication which becomes bound up in the child from day to day, and influences the dynamic self-manifestation of this human individual, in his or her narcissism, in relation to others and to self. In the case of a blessing, the person who pronounces the blessing initiates a loving act which appeals implicitly or explicitly to that person's idea of God, so that his or her religion, within the dynamic schema of the particular ethical system which he or she has adopted, conduces to a self-representation of that act of blessing as life-giving. To bless someone in God's name is to tell the person blessed that God chooses and sees that person as a distinct individual. The person pronouncing the blessing is as it were a witness to a choice which his or her love underwrites. I think the word 'blessing' has a theological meaning even if the person conferring a blessing knows nothing of theology.

2. PROPHETIC WORDS AT BIRTH

Pohier: That is true. Have you ever met with actual words of blessing or curses during your experience as a psychoanalyst?

Dolto: No, never. But I have found traces of words which have marked people indelibly. What midwives say during delivery can leave a very heavy mark. They brand the mother as much as the child. What is said during the first hours and the first days of life marks people fearfully. But it is possible to counteract that, to rework the effects. For instance, when talking to the mother to find out why this particular saying of that particular person could have had such an influence . . . How often I have heard prophecies: 'Aha! You'll see what a time he (or she) will give you!' The baby who, at the same time as its mother, hears that in the first hours of its life, is marked by it. That child (and I have seen such cases) will be a lasting source of concern for its mother. You find this in analysis. And when you explore together with the mother the reason why she set such high value on what another person said (in relation, that is, to everything else going on around her), you discover that the woman who prophesied bad luck was worn out when the future mother arrived at the hospital; that she was angry or nervous; and that the delivery started suddenly, and not when it was expected. She had every reason to be antipathetic, because she was in a state of stress, for example. So she said that about the baby, and that marked the mother, who in her turn probably swore at these words because she did not feel that the midwife had made her welcome. Midwives who have been kind and efficient with the mother before the moment of delivery have never been known to say these things. The culprits are always midwives unknown to the mothers, or who the mother has already had reason to feel have ill-treated her to some extent.

Pohier: The Bible contains many blessings which are proffered in the form of prophecies. God, or the angel of God, or a prophet picks out someone and announces a splendid or ghastly fate for that person. Is there any connection between blessing and prophecy?

Dolto: Yes, of course, there is Simeon and the *Nunc dimittis* . . . That is true. And it is true that something like that happens to many if not all children. All deliveries are accompanied by something like that, in the first words uttered by people on whom the mother, for one reason or the other, has to rely at that point. But that may show in the analysis of the child. It shows when, in the case of a connotation which may give rise to anxiety, the mother has understood that personal psychological reasons were behind what was said to her own father, her own mother, or someone who played the role of mother- or father-substitute, in that very special moment. The hours before and after delivery and the few days following the birth of a child are very special for the conscious and unconscious mind of a woman who is not in her usual balanced state. Birth, like death, borders on mystery, on the human enigma. What is remembered of moments of doubt, and logical commotion, may be reprocessed when they are re-lived during a cure, in the course of psychoanalysis. Those effects which led to a loss of dynamic intensity may be treated. But a curse! My own opinion is that there is a radical difference between what arises psychologically from the reciprocal influence of the parents' unconscious on the children's unconscious, in short what is desired, and what is consciously retained by the aversion to life of someone who utters a curse and who thus refers implicitly, if not explicitly, to God.

3. PRONOUNCEMENTS ABOUT FAMILY AND LINEAGE

Pohier: In the Bible, it happens that someone is cursed together with all his descendants because he has cast aspersions on the fate of a family, or a lineage, whether his own or another.

Dolto: Things like that are met with in analysis, in the case of autistic children, for instance. It is like a curse, but it is not uttered as such. These are obscure areas in the parents' narcissistic relations with themselves. These parents find that they had problems: the mother with her grandfather or grandmother, for example. And the child which she brings into the world experiences something like a lacuna in its relation to the individual who in its own structure is identified with that grandfather, grandmother, or whoever it was. This person is representative of the passive or active impulses in that child during a primitive moment of its life. In infantile psychoses, you find the *equivalent* of a 'curse-like' effect in descendants, sometimes emanating from a grandfather or a grandmother. You find that the second person in each of the families descended from this grandparent, two or three different cousins at the same age, are affected to a lesser or greater extent with psychosis. You can see that, if you look for it, in the lateral relatives of a person in analysis. It is very difficult to understand. Is it because the mothers, knowing one another, compared their babies with one another, as if they were not each the children of different fathers and mothers, therefore not to be compared other than in 'appearance'? Some babies at the breast and infants are especially sensitive to criticisms of their deep-lying selves. In these family games, the babies are detached from their actual origins and the context of their parents and their love for them, so that they can become objects, 'things' apart from their real family, for the purposes of comparison. They are separated in order to see who is the more beautiful in comparison with other babies and other children, and treated like dolls or pets, to see whether, perhaps, they show their mother to good advantage in comparison with the other mother.

Or (and this, I think, is more often the case) the person who has initiated the game (on one occasion it could be the grandfather, for instance), did something wrong or vile which caused the grandmother, his wife, to suffer and to react by retreating into shamed silence and a depressive state. This suffering is tacit and accompanied by anxiety, absence, and the least possible attention to her children: her daughter is marked by it, and the child of that daughter at the same age will be marked by it too. Until the thing which they concealed is discovered, until 'something nasty in the woodshed' is revealed, the grandfather or grandmother who has done whatever wrong thing it is, who has failed (in short, who has done something serious and unspeakable) and the silence which carries the shame and shortcoming, together produce a kind of devitalising dumbness. This infertile and sterile state affects an especially receptive child which is a member of that family, and certain impulses are never confronted in him or her, in the father or mother, by words which could make them meaningful, or by other impulses which might make them productive, or 'bear fruit'.

Pohier: 'Bear fruit'—that is the typical expression used in biblical blessings. You bless something or someone so that it or he or she will bear fruit.

Dolto: Yes, but the odd thing is the difference between the fruit as formulated by the person offering the blessing, and a fruit which is beyond what the person blessing and the person blessed might imagine. It's a chain reaction which brings happiness where blessing is concerned. It is something beyond the conscious suppositions of the agent and author of the blessing, and beyond what the person blessed might think of his or her own actions. Perhaps there is no effect for the present, but the person blessed says: 'It will be all right because my father (or my mother) told me that I would succeed. I shan't see it but my children will'. I myself have never observed secondary depressing thoughts following on actual curses, but at most quite superficial things such as questions of the order of 'Why have I been punished?' or 'What did I do to God?' But I have seen people who experience the burgeoning feeling of having been made quite confident about themselves and the future. They do not have much real present cause to believe that that will be the case, but they are convinced that it will be so eventually 'because that person told me and I trust him (or her)'. That thought supports people in difficult moments. Blessings are like bridges or ropes from one river bank to the other; they support those who trust themselves to them in order to cross the water to a spot where there will be no foothold.

4. BLESSING AND TOUCHING

Pohier: That reminds me of a form of liturgical blessing which has evolved considerably and which is still to be found with the transformation of extreme unction into the blessing of the sick. Does that function of comforting play a part?

Dolto: Yes, indeed it does, over and beyond the impotence of doctors. Doctors are always mother-substitutes. They always replace the woman who feeds her hungry child, washes her dirty child, and consoles and comforts a child in pain. Even though he or she may sometimes have a castrating function, a doctor always has a maternal function. Someone who surpasses a doctor is the person who acts with words alone, listening compassionately to statements and expressions of suffering, without doing anything substantial to this body which is being racked by anguish, and the silent condition of whose organs is actually a physiological disorder expressing the anxiety of the person in question. It is in the context of desire that listening to words and the utterance of words have their effect of reconciling the human being with his or her self.

Pohier: But in liturgical blessings, there is something more than words. Sacraments also contain something other than words. There are always gestures in blessings and sacraments, and I feel that these gestures, which almost always include some form of touching, are important.

Dolto: Yes, they are important, as recourse to a third element, water, oil, 'chrism', sometimes is. It is true that when a child that as yet has no concept of its body in a looking glass, knocks itself or burns itself, it goes to mother. The mother touches it (sometimes mother's touch leaves a trace in the form of some antiseptic ointment or other . . .) and there we are! All over! Perhaps there is still a big bump, but the child no longer complains, because Mummy has touched it. She has taken over. It is as if the child said: 'Since Mummy knows, it's all right. She has taken on me and my pain and I can rely on her.

She isn't anxious, and so I'm not worried about myself because Mummy isn't worried about me'. It is obvious that if the mother is worried because a child has fallen over and it has not even been harmed, the child will be marked by the incident all afternoon, because it has hurt its mother and the mother is anxious, and it may think that it is to blame. The blessing proves that the person bestowing it is worried neither by the person who is being blessed, nor by the relationship with him or her. The person receiving the blessing is wrapped neither in doubt nor in ambivalence, but in the love which wants to go on shining on him for a long time.

5. BLESSINGS ON A STATE OR FUNCTION

Pohier: What do you think of blessings which not only refer to a person but which sanction or promote a certain state or function? I am thinking, for example, of a 'nuptial blessing', or even the 'ordination' or 'consecration' of a priest.

Dolto: For marriage, it is necessary that each person involved should make an entirely free vow to the other. A blessing of that kind promotes a vow (which has the meaning of commitment, and a psychological and narcissistic dimension). It is a form of words which marks passage from one state to another, to a role in the world, and which radiates in the social world. Then, especially, it promotes that statement and intention by bestowing on it consequences exceeding what might be imagined, and by affecting the future of the person's sexuality, and therefore his or her descendants, which of course is the burden of the blessing on the young bride in the marriage ritual. As far as the ordination or consecration of a priest is concerned, it seems to be that there is above all a conveyance of power, which henceforward will be exercised through the mediation of this person through the medium of the duties with which he is charged, by the meaningful gestures of his body carrying out the ritual through which he maintains and transmits the dynamic meaning that it conceals, irrespective of the way in which that person conducts himself. The priest in his private and social person becomes the instance of projection and appeal for people who through that person mediating for them show they need God. This person who has been admitted to the priesthood receives the power to bless, because he becomes for the believers whom he blesses the representative of God's power and love.

Pohier: In the ordination ritual, there is a very impressive moment when all the priests present place their hands on the heads of the ordinands. This reminds me of the function of touching which you were speaking of just now.

Dolto: Yes, and those who make that gesture know that it is a gesture which, conveyed as it is from one person to another, goes all the way back to Jesus who himself gave power to his apostles. And there is also the blessing which parents give their children, which also consists of placing a hand on their head. I am actively concerned in running a place we call the 'Green House', where there are infants from birth to three years of age, who come with their parents to meet other children, to socialise in the security of the common tutelary presence of the parents. One very often sees the eldest child of less than three with a newborn brother or sister. At first the older child feels the pangs of the reaction known as jealousy, which means a kind of hesitation about their identity which is always connected with a certain quality of love. 'Which is better: to be a wailing infant or to be me?' to be a big person, which I am not yet, or to be a baby as I was? 'And then there is the question of whether one sex is more valuable than the other. It is a very difficult aspect of things for all human beings. Once it is all but resolved, when the child becomes less worried about its right to its own identity, it becomes more positive about its little brother or sister. I am very surprised to see the—unconscious—modes of behaviour in which it engages from time to time (whether it is a boy or a girl, and the baby similarly). It plays, approaches the baby, and lovingly places its chubby little hand for just a moment—for two or three seconds—on the baby's forehead, then it goes away. It generally puts its palm on the root of the nose and fits its hand over the forehead. Clearly the baby likes that, and often it smiles. These children do not have specially Catholic mothers. But even the non-Catholic mothers place their hand on their child's head to say: 'I have confidence in you. I give you confidence'. It is a lay blessing. The children like that, even when they are big (there is no age for blessing one's children!). Clearly, even *in utero*, this touching has marked the weeks of intimacy; when they were born they knocked against their mothers as they used their heads to try to find the way out for their bodies. This started the birth process and allowed them to escape a difficult moment. It was the start of contact with the body of the other person who, after having protected them within, becomes as it were an obstacle and undergoes the labour of delivery. Some part of all that is repeated when the same mother places a positive hand on the child's head, saying: 'Yes, I trust you, go along now!'

6. A 'DIABOLICAL' NEUROSIS. EXORCISM

Pohier: I am astonished that you have so little to say on the basis of your clinical experience about the way in which marks on the futures of a certain number of persons may have been made by the words uttered over them in the name of God, or in reference to God.

Dolto: No, I haven't. Perhaps there are psychoanalysts who see more people than I do who have been marked by a certain type of education in the name of Christianity. But I do remember a young boy who had been sent to me as a so-called 'diabolical hallucinatory neurotic'. This 13–14-year-old boy suffered from a frightful twitching. He could not do anything without his tic. It took him more than half an hour to enter my consulting room by this door. He would enter, draw back, begin again, and blow between these moves in order to fight whatever 'it' was that prevented him from entering. He blew, took off his jacket or whatever, blew while making as if to leave it there, picked it up, and began to blow again. It was an exhausting procedure. Something very interesting is that, at the St Anne Hospital, which was where he had come from after being in hospital for a few months, he had told his psychiatrist that it was the devil who was between him and objects. This doctor was very interested in these phantoms which he had termed a hallucinatory psychosis with a satanic theme. With me he never used the word 'devil'. Never. He was a caricature of pain and anxiety. I asked him: 'But what stops you taking your jacket off?' He said: 'I don't know . . .'. 'Why do you blow?'—'I don't know . . .'. He never said that it was the devil. He was completely cured but he never told me what he imagined to be behind the 'it' which stopped him from completing any action.

Now this boy was very deeply marked by the fact that he was born because of a gynaecologist's advice to his mother. (He was consciously unaware of everything to do with his conception). He was born as the result of fertilization by someone other than his father. His father was infertile. This father had been a deserted child himself, entrusted to State care, and brought up in institutions. He loved his wife very much and wanted a child one hundred per cent. On examining the husband and wife, the doctor discovered that it was the husband who was infertile, but did not tell him. The gynaecologist told the wife: 'If you want to make your husband happy in this way, find someone to give you a child. Artificial insemination is difficult and expensive, and your husband will have to know about it when he is asked for his permission as the other spouse.' Finally, she went to her hairdresser, whom she had known for ten years and he was quite willing to do this for her. She was also a very beautiful though very simple woman who worked hard. She never flirted with, desired, or loved this hairdresser. The hairdresser and his wife were a peaceful couple with two daughters. Once he had done this 'service' for his client, this man was very moved by the fact that he had given a boy to a woman whom he did not love. There was all this at the basis of this boy's story, and also a great attachment to his mother, and a real affection for his father, a very obsessional man and a workaholic.

Yet this boy never talked to me about the devil. But I am convinced that, given his odd behaviour, the psychiatrist at St Anne's must have said: 'But he's possessed!' (perhaps even without really thinking so). He influenced him by saying that it was the devil. This boy had no religious education, and his parents were atheists. So I do not know what the devil could have meant for him. He never breathed a word about the devil to me. I can say 'breathed' because he continuously 'breathed' and blew to avoid a danger connected with touching things. But he never mentioned the devil to me.

Pohier: When you speak of possession and breathing or blowing, I think of exorcisms, which belong to the same family as blessings and curses. Exorcisms include words, rites, gestures, sometimes touching. But in exorcism the devil is addressed by name; you give him orders, and call him 'accursed'. You curse the devil in order to bless the possessed.

Dolto: Did God curse the devil, Lucifer? Does it say that in the Bible? In any case, the prophets and others did not scruple to curse people in God's name. After all, to curse someone is to call down a divine curse. It is true that you are not obliged to believe that God obeys this summons. In fact, can God curse? Especially after Jesus? However, the people who heard God's curse called down on them were convinced that God had obeyed, and that it had happened. And they were sure that the effect was neither reversible nor eradicable. At least, through the words of a physician, even under hypnosis. I do not know that the exorcists succeeded in doing that. In any case, exorcisms are directed only at curses by minor spirits, not at curses by God. If such a thing exists, it is not eradicable. Chertok told me that people affected thus believe that this kind of curse can disappear only with their own bodies, as if it were inscribed in their flesh.

Pohier: Even without recourse to the devil, we often use a vast number of tragedies or myths which portray human beings as condemned to their dreadful fates by personalised as well as non-personalised forces.

Dolto: In that case I really think that it is a matter of the Freudian unconscious and communications between human individuals through the unconscious in the Freudian sense, implicit language before language using words and beyond words, between the child and its mother and father. That means that there is a very precocious pre-superego, which means too that at four months the child understands phonemes pronounced in its mother tongue, whereas before four months it understands all languages. Provided that the person speaking to it truly wishes to communicate to the child what he or she thinks and feels, in short to speak to it, it understands all languages. It probably intuits what is said to it in the form of communication from one psychism to another—it is a kind of telepathy of communication. Its mimicking is really meaningful if you watch it. After four months it understands its mother's language. Thereafter most of them no longer have, in the bucco-pharygeal muscles and their larynx, the means of modulating the phonemes of another language, whereas at birth the mouth of a human being contains all the possibilities of pronouncing all the phonemes of all human languages.

It is as if the ability to correspond at choice with the mother, father and members of its own family made it lose the ability to communicate in other languages. That is the choice of the loved one. You do not accuse what you do not choose; you do not oppose it and you are not receptive to it. You do not seek it out, you leave it alone. The same thing happens when giving a blessing: you choose someone, and focus on him or her in a certain direction; that person is as it were picked out by a light beam which illumines him or her in a special way. The one blessed is loved by the person bestowing the blessing, whereas—though you do not wish others any harm—they are indifferent to you, and you let them drop.

When cursing, you choose someone in hatred. That is what is different. It is choice or election in reverse. Its parents can do nothing for a child which has been cursed by someone else. The structuralisation of children's identity by the parents' unconscious is the same for them as for the child—quite unconscious. Whereas the blessing is conscious for the person bestowing it, and a curse is conscious on the part of the person making the declaration, and doing and wanting the injury. If parents in analysis hardly mention words of blessing, it is probably because that is something they really cannot talk about. One cannot talk about something which one is continuously in the process of enjoying. One talks of something which is lacking. You might say that a blessing 'plugged you in'. Once plugged in, you do not need to speak any more. You are someone who does not even know that you have been blessed. You do not know throughout your life, yet it is that which sustains you in everyday life. To some extent it is what Job seemed to be saying. He had been blessed and suddenly the blessing seemed to have been taken away, and that was a trial. The life-forces, and a desire for the happiness of the person I know to have been cursed, are continually struggling against this curse and cannot forget it. It is a never-ending struggle.

7. BLESSINGS AND 'POPULAR RELIGION'

Pohier: You know that we are witnessing a certain religious renewal which is called, more or less accurately, 'popular religion'. Requests for blessings play a considerable part in it. These are requests addressed to the saints, and especially to the Virgin Mary, and requests about people but also about objects (even armaments are blessed!). At the very extreme, there is a commercial trade in blessed objects. What do you think of that?

Dolto: Just now we were talking about what impelled one to turn to someone who one thinks is unafraid, in order to confide one's anxiety or suffering in that person, just as the child has its mother touch its lump (the mark of blows) and its wounds. That is very understandable. Even in regard to objects that have been blessed. It is a form of fetishism which is necessary for human beings. At the very beginning of its life when its mother is absent, a child needs to possess an object which represents her through its smell or touch, or by some association of ideas which are linked with that object: this ribbon or rag, for instance, is associated with the cloth which she put around the child's face when it was feeding, and which retains the smell of the mother and one's own smell—both at the same time. In the commercial exploitation of blessed objects or even *un*blessed things (is Lourdes water blessed?), no words are pronounced with the water which is sold. It is the water which comes from that place and represents the associations of ideas and feelings connected with the place. And, for every human being, water stands for what slakes thirst, and therefore for something that satisfies a fundamental lack. It is the element which is indispensable to the life of the body, and by association to the life of the human spirit which the body images in its needs and desires.

I think that these objects always to some extent represent their mother mixed up with themselves. Moreover, the idea of the Virgin is the idea of the virgin mother. It is a little like Sade's Justine: whatever you do to her she remains undefiled. That is what the wonderful image is for the child: the mother who is always whole and entire. Because its real mother sometimes is aggressive to it; she sometimes throws things at its head, cannibalises it, scolds it, cuffs it, gets angry with it, and tells it off. She is 'marked' by what she is. She is not an eternal virgin; she is not what the child would like her to be. She is represented by an idealised woman, as the child pictures its mother. It imagines her as perpetually phallic, a source of milk, a source of tenderness for the unhappy child; a comforter of hearts and always assuaging thirst, for ever smiling.

It is also quite normal to take one's suffering to the saints, to request their intercession (people ask for protection and beg a blessing from them, to some extent rather than from God). Human beings are in such an unpredictable world; it is so threatening or inexplicable that they need to get everything they can on their side, because they feel perpetually like children who have no adult to help them. They extrapolate the adult who is lacking and whom they need to people who are dead and who were models and have been idealised, and who were truly worthy. There is reason to believe that these people whose spirits are close to God will continue to do good to those who ask for their protection. As little Sister Thérèse said: 'I shall spend my heaven doing good on earth'. To do good: to bless is to do good. It means: 'I wish you well. I prophesy good for you. I shall think of you and I shall think only good things for you.' That is what it is, the assurance which a human being obtains from a blessing. This creates a core of self-confidence which has the great advantage of not exploiting feelings of blameworthiness. The human being feels perpetually guilty in regard to self. When he or she discovers the effects of his or her actions ('I should not have done that . . .'), and above all when he or she feels free. It is so difficult to live that feeling of freedom: One has only oneself to blame. When one has other people to blame, because one supposes it all depends on them (even though one prefers as a result not to feel that one is free), one feels protected.

One always ends up hitting against the mystery of one's own existence, the mystery of one's own desire to be born. Why, in a primitive scene between a male and a female embracing, did the being that I am take shape? A creature of desire that day after day has revalidated this contract of survival . . . because 'I' am here. That is what analysis aims at, beyond the parents. Why did that happen? There are so many parents who do a thousand things to have children and have none. And others who want no children but self-eliminating foetuses, and others who abort themselves (or let themselves be aborted). Here we are faced with the mystery of conception. The exercise of sexuality which is necessary for that purpose is not the key to human procreation. Desire and love and their creative utterances of joy are not rutting, or a laboratory fertilisation of two gametes *in vivo*.

Pohier: Perhaps that is why believers think that reproduction is a divine blessing.

Dolto: Yes, it makes it possible to plug this mystery into God by means of a blessing. It means to give rise to generations, and to carry on from the primal desire which made a human being. We are creatures of words. We beget with words; we look at ourselves as words imaged in a body, that of a loved person. Each of us is responsible every morning for renewing our acceptance of life in a body, and for assuming this life consciously (unconsciously for those who have had the experience). But in order to feel that one is blessed in one's own existence, I think that a reference-person is necessary. One cannot rejoice in oneself alone. Another person is necessary to offer us the certainty that our living has a meaning beyond our pleasure or suffering; that it accepts us and blesses us just as we are. We might say that someone who was accursed was someone who had to keep himself or herself alive, as it were, because of the curse, struggling against a feeling of rejection from day to day. There is no longer any need for proofs. He or she no longer experiences any doubts. Henceforth it is like that; he or she is accursed! I think that someone who has been blessed needs his blessing to be sustained. By whom? By encounters discovered in the course of life; chances, proofs . . . He or she has to have proofs that he or she is blessed. For Christians, Jesus Christ and his life, death, and resurrection are the proof that we are blessed, and never to be cursed—at least, not by God.

8. AN INDELIBLE BLESSING

Pohier: While reading the Bible, we see that in the first stages of the history of the people of Israel, when there was a blessing a stone was put down, so that an almost indestructible trace was deposited of the fact that a blessing had been given.

Dolto: Those animals that live in bands mark their territory with their excrement, and the territory of the band is controlled by a certain kind of rule of social life for animals living together. These landmarks using substances which come from the body and keep their particular mark (smell) tell other bands or groups about the links between the bodies of individuals in the horde that are affiliated to one another. Surely that has been 'sublimated' in the 'blessing stones' which mark spots where events have taken place. They mark a territory. Among human beings, their territory is marked by a way of life. Families are marked by a style of life that fits them. This life style is a kind of rhythm, scent, tactility, language when one communicates with one another in the same language: an accepted consensus concerning the rules and means of saying, doing, and reproducing life. Blessing once again goes ahead and surpasses. A blessing unites more people, in a more subtle, indeed much more subtle way, than all their sensory references engaged in the ethics and aesthetics of their private and social life. The blessing on such a day at such a place aims at transcendence. It is a symbolic expression of a pleasure and rejoicing beyond the here-and-now of bodies and people.

Pohier: Therefore we have to offer one another these signs or marks of the fact that we have been blessed and that we are united in the same blessing.

Dolto: Yes, that is what should happen when one says 'Thank you!'—Thank you!: Whenever we say thank you for something, we relate ourselves and others to God, beyond the actual relationship that we are living and so we punctuate our existence with transcendence. The term is on the way to a blessing. The most important thing for a Christian is baptism. People who are not baptised know that, and those who are baptised much more so. From my childhood I have always thought that it was very important to have been baptised. It seemed to me to be the blessing of all blessings. Many Christians are not aware that it is something important and is an ineradicable benefit.

To be baptised is an indelible blessing, and one on which one can rely. From the moment one is baptised one can count on this blessing, whatever difficult moments may ensure. 'Because you are baptised there is something ineradicable in the confidence which you may have in yourself, because God has had confidence enough in you to connect you with all other Christians, living, past and of the future, those who are still in embryo and those who are going to become Christians'. That is brought about by baptism. Baptism is what joins us to the heavenly water which feeds everyone on earth: the circulation of that water is the life of earthly creatures. The water linked in baptism to the word of Jesus names each one of us, and this naming word is for ever linked to the Trinity. Baptism is a blessing which joins us to the Trinity. It associates the existence of this human being here, now and beyond the decaying of the flesh, to the fertility of the spirit of love which circulates and enlivens the least of our actions, however unconscious we may be of that. It's rather extraordinary, isn't it?

Jean-Marie Tillard

Blessing, Sacramentality and Epiclesis

A RAPID glance through the index of the *Rituale Romanum* produced by Pope Paul V in the wake of the Council of Trent is very rewarding. The first section (1–7) deals with the sacraments. This is followed by a list of blessings. These consist not only of blessings concerned with what could be termed the framework of formally sacramental actions, such as the places and objects of cult, the altar and the sacred vessels and the extension of those actions to the sphere of such 'sacramentals' as blessed candles, holy water and sacred icons, but also the blessing of places, objects and possessions used in everyday life. There is, for example, a formula for the blessing of a house, a wedding chamber, a ship, a field, a vine and fruit. Pilgrims can be blessed as they leave on pilgrimage and on their safe return. There are also special blessings for special occasions to be given to groups of Christians. One has the impression that the whole of human life and all that relates to it is included within the framework of blessings.

This impression is strengthened when the long appendix added in 1935 during the pontificate of Pius XI and published in the pocket edition of the Ritual is examined. It contains all the blessings approved since the appearance of Pius V's *Rituale Romanum* and they are concerned with a vast number of beings, things and situations, including, for example, blessings for the sowing of seed and of wells, roads, libraries, factories, cattle, pregnant women, babies, sickbeds and mountaineering equipment. The fundamental intention of this section of the Ritual is revealed in one blessing in particular: a formula *ad omnia* that covers any new possibility. The whole of human life is clearly placed under God's blessing.

There is no doubt, of course, that this Ritual is out of date, and not only the new texts promulgated since Vatican II have made this clear, but also the obvious fact that its language and spirit are no longer in accordance with our contemporary idea of the relationship between God and the world. All the same, the great number of these blessings bears witness to the presence of an intuition of the *sensus fidelium* in the Christian consciousness and also to the fact that 'popular Christianity' is not the only evidence of that *sensus*.[1] The proof of this is to be found in the blessing at the conclusion of the liturgical offices of Lauds and Vespers and even more importantly in that which closes every celebration of the Eucharist. This indicates that, even when the Christian community has just received the supreme gift of God's love, a need is still felt to ask God for a blessing. The great number of these requests for a blessing in many Eastern rites shows clearly that this is 'not a negligible part' [sic] of the life of faith of the People of God.

1. BLESSING AND FAITH IN GOD—THE SOURCES OF THE EPICLESIS

There is, however, quite a bewildering number of formulae and the objects blessed are bewilderingly diverse. Sometimes verbs with deep theological implications are used. These include, for example, *sanctificare* and even *consecrare*,[2] and sometimes even, without any clear difference in meaning within the space of a few lines and both referring to the same action, either *benedicere* or *consecrare*.[3] Despite this, however, with the exception of the altar, where the rite is explicitly called a *consecratio*,[4] all these cases are classified under the heading of 'blessings'. It would seem that the idea of blessing is not at all precise and even borders on the equivocal. It is, however, very necessary to define it more precisely.

We can eliminate straight away the meaning of blessing that occurs widely in the liturgical traditions, namely the *berakah*, blessing God for his work and the wonders of his love. This is very close to, but not quite the same as a thanksgiving and aims to praise God and recognise his glory. It forms a very important part of Christian worship[5] and is one of the elements that is rooted in the biblical tradition, but it is not this aspect of 'blessing' that the Ritual is concerned with. The blessing that we are considering here is an intervention on God's part in favour of those who believe in him, a means of grace by which believers hope to receive a concrete mark of God's benevolence as the Father of Jesus Christ.

(a) From Adam to the Lord Jesus Christ—the Creator and the Spirit— Creation and Promise

It is quite remarkable how closely the creative work of God is associated with his blessing in the priestly account at the beginning of the book of

Genesis. God blesses the birds and the fishes, man and woman and the sabbath, which is the day when he finishes his work (Gen. 1:22, 28; 2:3; 5:2). After the Flood and after affirming his determination not to curse the earth again, God renews his blessing (9:1). It is worth noting that this blessing does not in any way throw doubt on what we would now call the profane aspect of God's creative work—on the contrary, it places it firmly within the profane sphere and it is clearly the aim of the biblical author that the gift of life, which is the summit of God's creation, should develop fully. When Abram is blessed (14:19; 24:1) and God promises that this blessing will continue in his offspring, who are called to a glorious future (12:2; 22:17), when Isaac and then Jacob are also blessed (25:11; 32:30) and when 'the Egyptian's house' is blessed because of Joseph (39:5), it is clear that the same perspective is in view. What is more, the last of these texts also makes it evident that 'the blessing of Yahweh was upon all that he had, in house and field'.

Asking God for a blessing, then (49:25), is not in any way the same as asking him to sacralise and therefore to short-circuit the laws of creation or, as we would say nowadays, to violate their profanity. The flocks, fields and barns that are blessed in Deuteronomy (28:1–13) do not cease to be what they have always been for man—the object of constant care, the result of exhausting work and the means of daily subsistence. They do not become the object of a miracle, sparing man his normal experience. Nor do they become consecrated things, removed in advance from ordinary human use and kept on one side for the exclusive service of God and thereby made sacred. Only a portion of what is blessed by God—the first-born males of the cow or the ewe (Deut. 25:19), the first-born male child (Exod. 13:1), the first sheaf and the first basket of fruit of the ground (Deut. 26:2–10) are reserved as an offering to God that will not be given back, as a sign (*sacramentum*) of his lordship. But this deuteronomic text concludes, it should be noted, with the words: 'you shall set it down before Yahweh your God, . . . and you shall rejoice in all the good which he has given to you and your house, you, the Levite and the sojourner among you' (26:10–11). God's blessing, then, is an assurance and a guarantee that the goods on which the fullness of life depends are possessed and enjoyed. They are material goods, but they also provide the framework for a climate of peace and joy. That climate is summed up in the word *shalom*, the essence of which is faithfulness to God's wishes.

Everything depends on faith in God's control of creation and his lordship over all things. Whether he blesses or does not give his blessing and even if he curses (Deut. 11:16–32; 23:5), Israel has to continue to have faith in the one who controls the forces that are spread across the universe. As the People of God, they have to believe that the creator and lord of all things, whose work is subject to a plan of love, can, in his freedom, show favour to those who believe in him and guarantee their well-being and success, especially if they are careful to do his will (Deut. 28:10–12).

The theological climate of the blessing therefore coincides to some extent with that of the prayer of petition and intercessory prayer, but it also points to God's way of acting in his relationship with men. It is the initiative that he takes to give those whom he has created, by the effect of his grace, the opportunity to enjoy life, which is his supreme gift, in communion with him, to have offspring, possessions and power and to live in peace. In worship, this blessing is manifested as God's answer to the explicit or implicit petitionary prayer made by believers (see Ps. 128:5). Normally, however, it is the expression of God's favour. For this reason, this blessing is normally pronounced by those who act as intermediaries between the unseen God and his People. These include Moses (Deut. 33:1), Joshua (Josh. 22:6–7), the king (1 Kings 8:14, 55–61) and, above all, Israel's priests (Lev. 9:22; Deut. 10:8; 21:5; 1 Chron. 23:13).

Israel's religion, but not only its religion, its faith was rooted in the certainty that there would be temporal retribution on this earth. God's blessing was therefore inevitably accompanied by 'promises' that were renewed again and again to the patriarchs. Even more than this, his blessing became the focal point of Israel's hopes and the heart of the people's liturgical life (see Ps. 128:1–6). In the *tephillah*, the daily prayer of intercession *par excellence*, the words of God's blessing are followed by a request for his blessing[6] and the whole prayer ends with the priest's blessing.[7] The universal structure of Jewish prayer generally can also be understood better in this perspective as can the fact that it passed into Christian prayer: God is reminded of his blessing reinforced by his 'promises' and spelled out in the holy books and on this basis he is implored to exert his power according to the logic of his word.[8] The liturgy takes the inevitable form of blessing God for his blessings and entreating him to ensure that the whole of man's life, both individual and collective, will continue to flourish under his blessing.[9] Ben Sirach's description of this is justly famous (50:1–24, and especially 20–24).

The importance of the blessing, then, is undeniable. Any attempt to reduce or eliminate it would be to deprive the mystery of grace of its connection with the creative work of God and even to refuse to recognise the relationship between salvation and creation. The fruit of salvation is, after all, the fulfilment of that blessing which is inevitably based on human life in all its depth. It is, after all, not so much the vine, the harvest or the livestock that is blessed by God or his priests as the believer (and his family), by giving him a splendid crop or magnificent livestock. The nuance is important, since material goods are both the signs and the ways of blessing. According to modern ways of thinking, they are the 'symbols' in the powerful sense given to this term.[10] The nuptial blessing contained within the Latin marriage rite is an interesting case of the 'symbolisation' of God's blessing in and through the goods of a peaceful, fertile and happy life that has entered into faithfulness to the love of God.

It is hardly surprising that the New Testament should reflect the same faith in God's blessing. Jesus was for the apostolic community the one in whom all God's promises reached fulfilment (*teleiosis*). The fact that Abraham's blessing was fully accomplished in Jesus after having rested on God's holy People was proof of the truth and faithfulness of the God of the Fathers. Mary, the mother of Jesus (Luke 1:42) and Jesus himself (Matt. 21:9; Mark 11:9, 10; Luke 1:42; 19:38; John 12:13) are declared blessed and this is clearly because of the great messianic *kairos*, in which what was anticipated and had taken shape in the blessing and the promises of the past came to maturity. All those who believe in Christ are included in Abraham's promise (Gal. 3:9) in such a way that his promise was also transferred in Jesus Christ to the pagans as well (3:14) and the whole of the inheritance also became theirs (1 Pet. 1:4; 3:9). The earliest Christian preaching was based on that certainty. Peter announced to the Jews that 'God, having raised up his servant, sent him to you first, to bless you' (Acts 3:26). Paul told the church in Rome: 'I know that when I come to you I shall come in the fullness of the blessing of Christ' (Rom. 15:29). Following Irenaeus' intuition, the Christian tradition believed that the blessing given to Adam had been 'recapitulated' in Christ (*anakephalaiosis*), along with that of the patriarchs of the People of God. Creation had then been 'accomplished' in and through the saving act of Christ and the whole of mankind, thanks to the 'sacramental' calling of the People of Abraham and to that of Jesus, 'of the race of Abraham', had entered into God's blessing, which henceforth presided over the whole of man's destiny.

The liturgy of the Christian Church cannot therefore be situated outside the framework of this 'mystery' of God's blessing. It is firmly rooted in the Jewish liturgy,[11] possibly more by being included within this deep faith in God's blessing than by its acceptance of certain ritual forms. At the centre of this faith is the celebration of the sacraments and that celebration is the special time at which a community of believers assembles to be blessed by God, the Father of the Lord Jesus Christ and to receive the fruit of that blessing through the Church's ministry. The Church is both the servant and the beneficiary of God's benevolent power. It is therefore clear that sacramental actions only exist in order to allow God's blessing to enter the lives of Christians and completely to fill them. The section of Paul's Letter to the Romans dealing with baptism bears witness to this (Rom. 6:1–23). All the Church's sacraments are 'symbols' (in the powerful sense of the term referred to above) of God's blessing. It is not merely by chance that the materials used in them should be the water, the bread and the wine of a meal and oil. The blessing given to Adam is included in that of Christ Jesus and follows the way of creation.

Under the New Covenant, however, the place of the object of the blessing and the content of the promise is transcended, although attention is still given to the possession of the goods of creation. The summaries in the Acts of the Apostles stress that 'there was not a needy person among them' (Acts 4:34) because the members of the early Christian community 'had everything in common'. This is because the aim of these summaries was to show that the early Church was still subject to God's blessing, which meant that it was intolerable that any of the 'brethren' should be in need (see 1 John 3:17; James 2:15–16). This accounts also for the repeated insistence on the principle of almsgiving to be found especially in the Lucan writings (see Luke 6:30; 11:41; 12:33; 16:9; 18:22; 19:8; 21:1–4; Acts 9:36; 10:2, 4, 31; 11:29; 24:17).

In Luke's gospel, a statement about the kingdom of God is followed by one about the need to trust God and not to be anxious about the cares of this life (Luke 12:22–32; see Matt. 6:25–33). These words can be seen as an expression of a conviction that the Kingdom implies a continuation of God's blessing including the goods needed for human subsistence. Nonetheless, texts of central importance such as the beatitudes, the original significance of which is apparently preserved in the Lucan version,[12] and the parable of the rich young man who wanted to follow Christ (Luke 6:20–26; 18:22) also show quite clearly that the blessing transcends those realities, such as material possessions, a good reputation, harmonious relationships with one's fellow-men and *joie de vivre*, that normally form the fabric of human happiness. It is, in other words, possible to find possessions in poverty and weeping (6:20) or at least a guarantee of the kingdom and the way to it (18:24–30).[13] Possession of the eschatological goods of 'eternal life' is the authentic fulfilment of that blessing in the kingdom that is to come.

The Power of the Spirit

The ultimate object of the blessing, which was sensed by the prophets, who made it the content of the promise (Joel 3:1–5; Zech. 4:6; 6:8; Ezek. 36:27; 37:14), has been known since Pentecost—it is the Holy Spirit. As Paul told the Galatians, the blessing of Abraham is summed up in the Spirit (3:14). He also told the Romans that God's faithful love and the whole of divine grace have been 'poured into our hearts through the Holy Spirit' (Rom. 5:5). In his Letter to the Ephesians, he also speaks of 'every spiritual blessing' (Eph. 1:3).

It is in this 'spiritual blessing' that the fullness of God's gift from which all the rest comes and which is the fullness of Christ is to be found (see Eph. 1:3; Gal. 3:14). The Spirit of blessing is in fact the Spirit of Christ. The risen Lord, however, is not simply the one who was found by apostolic faith to be the expected Messiah, the *Christos* whom the promise had in mind. He is also seen to be intrinsically linked with the work of creation itself and God's first blessing. The canticle contained in the Epistle to the Colossians, which is in all probability based on the Wisdom literature (see Prov. 8:22–30), claims that 'in him all things were created' (Col. 1:16) and this is echoed in the Letter to the Hebrews (1:1–3; see 11:3), the Prologue to the fourth gospel (John 1:3) and even Paul's First Letter to the Corinthians (1 Cor. 8:6).

Entering by faith and the sacraments into the death and resurrection of Christ and becoming a 'member of his body' or a 'branch of the vine' is equivalent to entering into a blessing from which the goods of creation are not absent, but in which they form part of a more radical gift, that of the Sprit. Seized in this way by the Spirit, they become as it were enclosed within the communion with what is most precious to God himself, his own life, his agape. What is more valuable than anything else, then, is the quality of the person, the 'image' that can, as the Fathers claimed in their interpretation of Genesis, lead back to the 'likeness'. There is, however, no necessary connection between an accumulation of possessions beyond man's needs and the most profound truth of human life. Some forms of possession can even tarnish or compromise that truth and the profundity of the human person. God's benevolence is sought in the liturgy and at the same time the Spirit is asked to give the believer that quality of life, while the profane nature of material goods is respected. These goods are sometimes even demanded, but they are always submitted to that mysterious 'communion' with God, of which he is the agent. The entire sacramental liturgy is in fact a form of *epiclesis*. It is, in other words, centred on an appeal to the Holy Spirit, who is asked to acquaint believers with the blessing of which he made Christ the bearer at the resurrection (Rom. 8:11) so that it would be handed on by him to 'many' (5:15).[14]

(b) The Aim and Meaning of the Liturgical *Epiclesis*

I have gone to some lengths to outline the theology underlying the liturgical *epiclesis* that is either explicitly or implicitly present in all the emphatic aspects of the sacramental liturgy.[15] This is because I wanted to show that it is not simply one rite among others. The *epiclesis* is the supreme prayer of faith and the moment in the celebration of the liturgy when there is direct contact between God's blessing (as 'recapitulated' in Christ) and the believing community. It is therefore because of the *epiclesis* that the liturgy of the Church has become more than simply a religious act or purely a means of sacralisation with little contact with the authentically imperative needs of life in the world. The prayers of the *epiclesis* may not always be closely linked to a long reminder or *anamnesis* of the great steps in the history of God's blessing of his People,[16] following the model of the eucharistic anaphoras or the prayers of consecration for the baptismal font. They are, however, all steeped in faith in God's work, a faith which combines as one and indivisible both God's creation and his salvation on the one hand and his blessing of Adam and that of Jesus Christ on the other.[17] In a word, the *epiclesis* asks that 'the object of our faith—the God of the patriarchs who has blessed us in Christ—may be fulfilled *hic et nunc* in us'. That is the meaning, for example, of the Egyptian eucharistic epiclesis of Saint Mark: 'Fill, O God, this sacrifice of blessing which comes from you with the visit of your very Holy Spirit'.[18]

A careful examination of a number of different liturgies and their historical development, then, throws a clearer light on the situation. In those cases in which the *epiclesis* asks for the Spirit to bless both the realities used in the rite and persons, this is done following a hierarchy of values, the persons being primarily and essentially kept in mind. What is more, the earliest eucharistic *epicleses* do no more than simply implore God to send his Spirit down on those who believe.[19] Action concerning the elements is subordinated to this blessing.[20] The *anaphoras* of the Roman Missal of Paul VI, in which the account of the institution, preceded by the prayer for the Spirit, is inserted between the two parts of the *epiclesis*, as in the Egyptian tradition,[21] also ask for the bread and wine to become the Body and Blood of Christ 'for us'.[22]

The same applies to the liturgy of baptism. The Syriac rite contains this prayer, which is situated in the middle of the blessing of the water: 'Lord, who sent the Spirit on your only Son, God and Word . . ., may it please you to make your Holy Spirit descend at this moment on this your servant who is to be baptised'.[23] Perhaps more typical is the *epiclesis* over the chrism, of which there is evidence in the earliest traditions and which is echoed in the Gallican liturgies.[24] In this *epiclesis*, there is a prayer that, through the coming of the Holy Spirit, the chrism may become the garment of incorruptibility.[25] The underlying thought here is of the gifts of the new life and the 'putting on of the new man' (Eph. 4:22–24; see 1 Cor. 15:53–54; Col. 3:9–10), that is to say, that the 'new man' who, reaching fullness, is created by the benevolence of God among those who have entered into communion with Christ.

Finally, I would like to mention the interesting Byzantine *epiclesis* of the ordination of deacons: 'by the descent of your holy and life-giving Spirit, since grace is given to those who are worthy of you by the visit of your mercies and not by the laying on of hands, fill with a full faith, charity, power and holiness your servant who is present here'.[26]

It is obvious therefore that the liturgical actions together with their sacred content are directed towards the good of believers in the whole fabric of their existence. What is more, this 'sacred' aspect, including the case of the Body

and Blood of the one whom the Spirit has 'consecrated' Lord and Christ
through his resurrection, is clearly destined to bring believers into contact with
the blessing in which the gifts that God has given man since his creation are
recapitulated. That is why the *epiclesis* has always been followed in the great
anaphoras by a prayer of intercession. The latter is often very long and lists in
detail the main needs of the Christian community both in the spiritual and in
the temporal order. As for persons, they are seen as a whole.

The details of these intercessory prayers are quite important in this context.
The anaphora of Saint James, for example, contains a prayer for the holy
places, the church of Jerusalem and all the churches, ministers, virgins and
monks. There is also, however, a prayer asking God to remember the city, the
district, the civil rulers in their warlike dealings with their neighbours, sailors
and travellers, prisoners, exiles, those who suffer torture, the sick and the aged.
Finally, there is a prayer for rain, clement weather, the harvests and a fruitful
year 'crowned with your good gifts'. The whole intercession ends by imploring
the one who 'has lordship over life and death' to 'remember' all believers 'for
earthly and heavenly goods, corruptible and incorruptible riches and what is
temporal and what is eternal'.

This list of prayers, which is very reminiscent of the Eastern Orthodox
prayer for Good Friday, is a summary of what is revealed by Scripture as the
content of God's blessing from Adam to Christ, that is from creation to the
resurrection, in which God's 'first work' is included and its balance restored.
All the essential aspects can be found in the anaphoras of the Eastern
Church.[27] It is hardly necessary to point out that, in the quite unique complex
of which Christian initiation consists, it is in the intercession that forms part of
the eucharistic anaphora that the content of the gift made in Jesus Christ is
detailed. That gift is made, in the words of the prayer of consecration of the
waters contained in the Euchologion of Serapion,[28] to those who have in
baptism entered into the action in which God 'spares (his) work, saves the
creation that is the work of (his) hands' and enables believers 'to be fashioned
in the image of (his) divine and inexpressible beauty'.

The *epiclesis* of the celebration of the Eucharist, then, as the central act and
the highest point of the Christian liturgy, is also essentially concerned with the
goods of creation. These have their own special place, but in a very real sense
they form part, as profane realities, of God's blessing as fulfilled in Christ. The
blessings of the Ritual, the most important of which are contained in the
intercessions of the *anaphora*, are theologically derived from this central act of
the Eucharist, rather as an *explicitation or extension of that act*. This is true
whatever the situation may be with regard to the history of the rites. It is well
known that they go back a long way in the history of the liturgy, possibly even
to its origins.[29] As for their meaning at the deepest level, they therefore have

nothing to do with an excessive desire to give profane and earthly realities a sacral value nor does superstition play any part. They are rooted in a deep faith in the 'recapitulation' of God's blessing in Jesus Christ.

2. GOD'S BLESSING AND THE THEOLOGY OF THE RITUAL

A New Look

I have already referred to a certain difference between contemporary theology and the content of the Roman Ritual. I said that the language and thought of the latter was no longer in accordance with our way of interpreting the relationship between the Creator and his creation. If what I have said so far in this article is correct, it is obvious that this uneasiness cannot be traced back to the underlying intention and explanation of the blessing. We have already seen that, in Christ, all the goods of creation entrusted to the 'image of God' are included within God's blessing, although they are orientated towards and subordinated to the spiritual goods. Blessings of persons, as we have seen, cause no serious difficulties.

The difficulties come in the first place from a certain change of position. An earlier conviction that believers could be 'blessed in their goods' has given way to the idea that the goods themselves could be blessed. Origen was farseeing enough to recognise this problem. If Theophilus, the Bishop of Alexandria, who is known to us through one of Jerome's letters (*Ep*. 98, 13; *PL* 22, 801), is correct, he doubted the effectiveness of the Spirit with regard to inanimate objects. This doubt is also apparent in some of his own statements.[30] In this question of blessing such material objects, the created realities used as the 'matter' of the sacraments and therefore not performing their normal function (the bread and wine used at the Lord's Supper, the water of baptism and the oil of the chrism) and indeed all objects used in cult and therefore deprived of their purely profane use form a special case and have to be considered separately. The urgent question is: Why should a vine, a house or the sea be blessed or, as in the supplement to the 1935 edition of the Ritual, a bridge or an electric turbine? Surely these all have their ordinary use. Why, then, bless them?

There is only one really valid answer to this question and this can be more readily understood if we consider it in the light of the contrast with the nuptial blessing, which is centred on the bride. Blessing a thing on the basis of the profane use that is made of it really means that we are asking God to continue to protect all those who use it for as long as the thing itself lasts. The formula or the act of blessing is therefore a concrete way of denoting firstly the object of the request and secondly the continued nature of the protection that God is asked to give. As long as this bridge exists, we pray, as long as this sea is a highway and as long as this house stands, may anyone who crosses it, sails on it or lives in it do so without danger and be blessed. The emphasis is therefore clearly on persons and God's blessing is sought for them.

There is, however, another reason for the present difficulty. For some years now we have been looking at the realities of creation in a different way from the way that we looked at them in past centuries. We are conscious that created realities have a certain autonomy and that God himself respects the laws of the universe that he has created and lets it evolve in accordance with its own forces. We no longer think of the rain and the harvest, storms and natural disasters as being 'in the hands of Providence' as Christians did in the past and know that some interventions bordering on interferences with secondary causes sound like miracles. The prayers of the Ritual do not, however, ask for miracles.

The twentieth-century Christian has consequently made himself responsible for many of his anxieties and concerns about the destiny of his world and believes that he can enter into dialogue with God and be converted to his plans. He is convinced that peace and happiness in human society will above all be the result of a more just distribution of the goods of this earth and a more correct use of power, since man now has or will acquire the technical means to remedy the shortcomings of nature.

The biblical teaching about man as made 'in the image of God' has also been seen in a new light by contemporary Christians. In the language of the book of Genesis, 'image' means 'vizier', *chargé d'affaires*, a person bearing a responsibility which is given to him by God and from which he cannot withdraw. The future of the world is therefore entrusted to man as a being whose intelligence has to be applied to the task in conjunction with his heart. In this way, it comes within the category of God's grace and its ability to change men's hearts and therefore fully within the sphere of the blessing in the evangelical sense. It is, of course, true that the creature whom Pascal saw as very small in contrast with the star-filled space of heaven will always feel in one way or another at the mercy of the obscure and ungovernable forces that control the universe. All the same, if he is to conserve his earth subject to God's blessing, he must have the courage to seek and an upright conscience.

The period in which we are living will no doubt go down in history as the one in which there has been an almost universal increase in our desire that all men should have sufficient goods and that the latter should be fairly distributed. Christians have devoted a great deal of their time and energy to this task, opting courageously for the poorest people in the world and working to improve their situation. This means that asking for God's blessing, especially in the sphere of man's relationship with the material goods of creation as seen in the light of the scriptural teaching outlined in this article, once again has a place in Christian experience. This emerges quite clearly, for example, from even a cursory study of the liturgies and prayer books used by certain communities in Latin America or Asia. The poor and the oppressed are beseeching God to 'turn his face towards them'.

It is obvious, of course, that the first blessing for which God is asked should be that our hearts should be 'visited by the Spirit'—that the hearts of those in power should be blessed with a blessing of justice and compassion and that those of the poor should be blessed with a blessing of solidarity, sharing and courage. It is more important to look for blessing in that area than in the sphere of places of work, tools and harvests. If, however, it is agreed, in order to respect the wishes of many of the poorest communities with a firm attachment to traditional rites, that the places where people live and work should be blessed, then it should be clearly understood that God is in fact asked to bless these places and things so that everything may be done in and with them according to his plan. If this is not stressed, there is always a danger of falling into folklore and magic.

The Nature of the Blessings

The blessings of the Ritual can now be seen in their real light. If we accept that the *epiclesis* is primarily concerned not with 'consecrating' certain realities, but with persons, then we can see that these blessings have to be regarded as an extension of the *epiclesis*. They do not bring about any change in the reality of things, as the eucharistic *epiclesis* does in the case of the bread and wine. Nor do they make them into 'sacred' things completely removed from the sphere of ordinary profane use, on the model of the *epiclesis* pronounced over the chrism. If they do happen to do this, it is always in connection with a celebration of a sacrament, in which the objects 'consecrated' in this way are included. They are above all invocative and set a seal on an appeal made to the Spirit for the continued use of a certain reality or, in the case of a blessing invoked for a person, for a certain situation, such as sickness or virginity, or for a certain activity, so that the person or persons concerned may be subject to the effective operation of God's blessing. In this way, they objectivise faith in God's absolute lordship over all things and in the certainty of his love. They also indicate that God will, by virtue of his promise, continue to protect with his grace those for whom the rites have been celebrated. It is not possible to say whether the objects or the persons for whom a blessing is sought have a special power derived from God, as in the case of the strictly sacramental *epiclesis*, but the blessings of the Ritual certainly define and to some extent denote the sphere in which God is asked to make his blessing manifest.

The Ritual of the blessings therefore forms part of the sacramental order. My examination of this question has of necessity been very rapid because of the restricted length of this article, but it has shown that, within this sacramental sphere, the goods of creation cannot be regarded simply as signs of grace with only the supernatural life or eschatological realities in view. Creation has not been cancelled out by the resurrection. God, the Father of Jesus Christ, continues to be the one who gave the earth to Adam for his happiness and it is that gift that the Ritual of the blessings 'symbolises', in other words, makes manifest and explicit for faith, since the whole question of blessing has to do with faith.

Translated by David Smith

Notes

1. It would not be difficult to show how the middle ages were marked by this *sensus*. It is also to be found in the Eastern Orthodox world, but the forms of expression there are different.

2. Examples are the priest's vestments, the altar cloths, the corporals and so on; see Tit. 8, Cap. 20, 21, 22.

3. See, for example, the case of the chrism in the *Instructio pro simplici sacerdote sacramentum confirmationis ex Sedis Apostolicae delegatione administrante*, Nos. 3 and 4.

4. No doubt because of the 1917 *Codex Iuris Canonici*, Canon 1200.

5. For the *berakah* used in this sense, see J. P. Audet 'Esquisse historique de genre litteraire de la benediction juive et de l'Eucharistie chrétienne' *RB* 65 (1958) 371–399; *ibid.* 'Genre litteraire et formes cultuelles de l'eucharistie' *Eph. Lit.* 80 (1966) 353–385; *ibid. La Didachè, instructions de Apotres* (Paris 1958); L. Bouyer *Eucharistie théologie et spiritualité de la prière eucharistique* (Tournai 1968); H. Cazelles 'L'Anaphore et l'Ancien Testament' *Eucharisties d'Orient et d'Occident* I (Paris 1970) pp. 11–21; *ibid.* 'Eucharistie, bénédiction et sacrifice dans l'Ancien Testament' *MD* 123 (1975) 7–28; B. Fraigneau-Julien 'Eléments de la structure fondamentale de l'Eucharistie, I. Bénédiction, anamnèse et action de grâces' *RSR* 34 (1960) 35–61; C. Giraudo *La struttura letteraria della preghiera eucaristica* (Rome 1981); P. Jouon 'Reconnaissance et remerciement en hebreu biblique' *Bibl* 4 (1923) 381–385; *ibid.* 'Reconnaissance et action de graces dans le Nouveau Testament' *RSR* 29 (1939) 112–114; R. J. Ledogar *Acknowledgement, Praise-Verbs in the Early Greek Anaphora* (Rome 1968); L. Ligier 'Les Origines de la prière eucharistique, de la Cène du Seigneur à l'Eucharistie' *QLP* 53 (1972) 181–202; T. J. Talley 'De la Berakah à l'eucharistie, une question à réexaminer' *MD* 125 (1976) 11–39.

6. C. Giraudo, in the work cited in note 5, pp. 224–231, has studied this text and provided a Latin translation of it; see 227; for line IX, 62, he gives: 'Benedic super nos, Domine Deus noster, annum istum in bonum'.

7. *Ibid.* 224, n. 44.

8. *Ibid.* 362 and n. 18; see also *ibid.* 159 with the interesting example of Acts 4:24–30.

9. S. Mowinckel *Psalmenstudien V. Segen und Fluch in Israels Kult und Psalmdichtung* (1923) 130 has provided a synthesis of this overlapping of the two blessings, *berakah* as blessing God and *berakah* as God's blessing of man.

10. See my contribution to *Initiation à la pratique de la théologie* III (Paris 1983) pp. 392–403.

11. This has been clearly shown by F. Gavin *The Jewish Antecedents of the Christian Sacraments* (London 1928); J. Heinemann *Prayer in the Talmud* (Berlin and New York 1977); W. O. E. Oesterley *The Jewish Background of the Christian Liturgy* (Oxford 1925); C. P. Price 'Jewish Morning Prayers and Early Christian Anaphoras' *AThR* 43 (1961) 153–168; J. Vellian 'The Anaphoral Structure of Addai and Mari compared to the Berakoth preceding the Shema in the Synagogue Morning Service contained in the Seder R. Amram Gaon' *Mus* 85 (1972) 201–223. See also J. Bouyer, the work cited in note 5 and J. T. Talley, the article cited in note 5.

12. See J. Dupont's fundamental work *Les Béatitudes* (Paris 1969–1973) vol. III.

13. See the excellent study by S. Legasse 'Pauvreté' *DSp* 613–634.

14. Irenaeus says this with his customary depth of thought: 'The Spirit came down on the Son of God who had become the Son of man in order to become accustomed with him to dwelling in the human race and living among men, to dwelling in God's work in order to bring about in those men the will of the Father and to renew them, changing their disuse into the newness of Christ . . . The Spirit (at Pentecost) led back to unity all the distant nations and offered to the Father the first-fruits of all the peoples. That is also why the Lord promised to send us the Paraclete, who adapts us to God', *Adv. haer.* 3, 17, 1–2.

15. See A. G. Martimort's study 'L'Esprit Saint dans la liturgie' *Atti del Congresso Internazionale di Pneumatologia* (Rome 1983); the collective study *Le Saint Esprit dans la liturgie* (*Eph. Lit.* 8, Rome 1977); E. G. Cuthbert and F. Atchley *On the Epiclesis of the Eucharistic Liturgy and in the Consecration of the Font* (Alcuin Club 31) (Oxford 1935).

16. C. Giraudo, in the work cited in note 5, who shows, especially in his synthesis, 357–360, this movement from the *anamnesis* (with its discourse in the indicative mood) to the *epiclesis* (discourse in the imperative). I would insist more emphatically than Giraudo on the way *anamnesis* with its reminder of 'God's action' penetrates the *epiclesis*.

17. The fourth anaphora of the Missale Romanum of Paul VI is very typical. Its Eastern origins are well known. Despite the brevity of the present blessing of the baptismal font, it still reiterates the essential aspects of the divine blessings given by the waters in the history of salvation. For tradition, see especially B. Neunheuser 'De benedictione aquae baptismalis' *Eph. Lit.* 44 (1930) 194–207, 258–281, 369–412, 455–492.

18. F. E. Brightman *Liturgies Eastern and Western* I (Oxford 1896) p. 132; A. Hanggi and I. Pahl *Prex eucharistica* (Fribourg 1968) pp. 116–127.

19. See L. Bouyer, the work cited in note 5, pp. 181–185, 204–212.

20. The earliest petition was for the Spirit to 'manifest' in the elements the Body and Blood of Christ (as in Basil's *anaphora*). The next petition was that he should 'make' of the bread and the cup the Body and Blood of Christ (the *Anaphora* of Saint James and Cyril of Jerusalem *Catéchèses mystagogiques* V, 7) and finally there was the petition that he should 'transform' the elements (the *anaphora* of John Chrysostom). The formula used in the *Anaphora* of Saint James is worth noting: 'Send that Holy Spirit into us and into our oblations, so that his coming . . . may sanctify this bread and make of it the sacred Body of Christ'.

21. See note 18 above.

22. *Anaphora* No. 2, Reconciliation No. 1.

23. See G. Khouri Sarkis 'Prières et cérémonies du baptême dans l'Eglise syrienne' *Orient Syrien* 1 (1956) 156–184, which should be read in parallel with S. Brock 'A New Syriac Baptismal Ordo attributed to Timothy of Alexandria' *Mus* 83 (1970).

24. See Joseph L. Levesque's illuminating study 'The Theology of the Post-baptismal Rites in the Seventh and Eighth Century Gallican Church' *Eph. Lit.* 95 (1981) 3–41; see also A. Chavasse 'La Bénédiction du Chrême en Gaule avant l'adoption integrale de la Liturgie romaine' *Revue du Moyen Age Latin* 1 (1945) 109–128; L. Mitchell *Baptismal Anointing* (Alcuin Club 48) (Oxford 1966); J. Quasten 'The Garment of Immortality. A Study of the *Accipe vestem candidam*' *Miscellanea Liturgica in onore di Sua Eminenze il Cardinale Giacomo Lercaro* (Rome 1966) pp. 391–401.

25. For the Eucologion, see J. Goar *Euchologium* pp. 502, 503. For the Gallican rites, see L. Levesque, the article cited in note 24, 17–23, 29–30, 42–43; A. Chavasse, the article cited in note 24, 112–113.

26. This text can easily be approached via E. Mercenier *La Prière des églises de rite byzantin* 1 (Chevetogne 1948) 374.

27. The sober tone of the Syriac Anaphora of the Twelve Apostles has been stressed by Dom Engberding.

28. This prayer contains a petition that the waters should be 'filled with the Holy Spirit', but it should be noted that it is addressed to the Logos, as in the eucharistic anaphora in the same euchologion.

29. See Hippolytus' *Apostolic Tradition* and the euchologion of Serapion, which also contains blessings of oil, cheese, new fruits, bread and water.

30. See *De Princ.* 1, 3, 5, 7.

Josep Lligadas

The Doctrine of Blessing in the New Roman Ritual

THIS ARTICLE will analyse the new Roman ritual *De benedictionibus*,[1] the most extensive of the rituals published in the wake of the conciliar reform.

The book begins with preliminary remarks (*Praenotanda*), after which the various formulas of blessing are divided into five parts, according to a classification which will be examined later. The categories are: persons, buildings and objects destined for the use of the faithful, things and objects used in churches, objects of popular devotion, and general formulas.

1. THE THEOLOGY OF THE *PRAENOTANDA*: WHAT IS A BLESSING?

The *Praenotanda* of the ritual begin with an attempt to define the meaning and value of the rites of blessing proposed. What this means is a presentation of God's blessing on human beings as effected through the history of salvation. The starting point is God, the source of all blessing and blessed above all things, who has done all things well and filled all his creatures with blessings. This God sent us his Son, who is his greatest blessing for human beings, and who is seen in the gospels transmitting this constant blessing of God. God finally completed his blessings with the gift of the Spirit. All this, say the *Praenotanda*, has been given effect down through the history of salvation, beginning with the covenant with the chosen people, the sign and sacrament of God's blessing for the world.

At this point, in contrast with the previous outline, is the following: 'God, from whom all blessing proceeds, even in those times granted people, particularly patriarchs, kings, priests, levites and fathers, the power to praise and bless his name and in his name to fill with blessings other human beings and created things.' These blessings 'promise some specific help from the Lord', announce his grace and proclaim his faithfulness to the covenant (*Praenotanda*, 8).

What this section does is to contrast the meaning of blessing just outlined, the realisation of the presence of God through creation as a whole and especially through salvation history, with this 'power to bless', which seems to present a different form of God's presence.

A more unified outline would be more consistent in drawing the implications of God's blessing in the new covenant. The Word made flesh began the sanctification of all earthly entities with the mystery of his incarnation, and after him the Church, following his teaching, gives thanks to God for his paschal mystery, which is shared with us in the Eucharist, and from the mystery of the Eucharist the Church draws grace for itself and the world and, in its role as the universal sacrament of salvation, performs among and for human beings the work of sanctification.

This ministry of sanctification is expressed in many ways by the power of the holy Spirit, and consequently 'the Church has instituted many forms of blessing, through which it calls upon human beings to praise God, urges them to ask for his protection, exhorts them to earn his mercy by holiness of life, and uses prayers to obtain his favours, so that its prayers may be happily answered' (*Praenotanda*, 9).

In terms of this presentation, the rites of blessing would be a making visible of God's saving presence in all worldly realities and of the ecclesial mediation of this saving presence. Accordingly the appropriate form for bessings would be a celebration of the word with prayer by the whole community (*Praenotanda*, 20–21) and efforts should be made to avoid the reduction of the blessing to a mere external sign (especially the sign of the cross) without any reading of the word of God or the saying of any prayer, because of the danger that this may encourage superstition and does not encourage the participation of the faithful (*Praenotanda*, 27). In the development of this idea, it is stated that blessings are acts of praise to God and petitions for grace 'with human beings and for human beings', and that, while the Church also blesses things and objects destined for liturgical life and human activity, in doing so it keeps in mind the people who will use the objects or act in the places (*Praenotanda*, 12).

This caution is reinforced in the chapter on 'Blessings for various circumstances' by a remark intended to exorcise regrettable or at least inconsistent practices of the past: 'Not everything should be used as an occasion to celebrate a blessing, not for example the inauguration of a monument or the preparation or presentation of instruments of war.'

The theme, as noted above, is the making visible ecclesially of the saving presence of God, a presence directed to human beings, which can also be seen as present in anything which is significant and contributes to the growth of human and Christian life according to the gospel (*Praenotanda*, 13). However, this line of argument runs into difficulties when the author of the *Praenotanda* tries to be more specific. The author here feels obliged to refer to specific 'effects' of blessings, without however being able to explain what they consist of. The impression created is of someone trying to preserve traditional statements about sacramentals, without being able to link them organically to the immediately preceding general theological statements. For example, the author of the *Praenotanda* (9–10) cites and applies to the present case general statements from the liturgical constitution of the Second Vatican Council ('Material signs signify and, each in its own way, bring about the sanctification of human being's, *Lit.*, 7). He then quotes what the constitution says about sacramentals: 'They are sacred signs created on the model of the sacraments by which effects, mainly of a spiritual kind, obtained by the prayer of the church are expressed', 60. But there is no further explanation. What was doubtless sufficient in a conciliar constitution, placed here as an introduction to a ritual of blessings proves insufficient—or unnecessary. In a ritual of blessings either there should be more explanation of what these particular 'effects' consist of (which would mean embarking seriously on the uncertain theme of the efficacy of sacramentals) or discussion should stop with the general theological outline already given, which was quite adequate. Apart from the conciliar texts, the only additional comment here is 'According to ancient tradition, the formulas of blessing are intended primarily to glorify God for his gifts and ask his favours, and to check the power of the evil one in the world' (*Praenotanda*, 11) which, stated in these terms, is not very enlightening. Clearly Christians advert to the power of evil in the world and invoke God's strength to resist it, but what does it mean to say that blessings are intended 'to check the power of the evil one in the world'?

2. WHO BLESSES?

According to the 1949 *Enciclopedia Cattolica*, 'Beautiful and moving though it may be, the blessing of children by their parents is no more than a private act, not an act of the Church.'[2] This is no longer the case. Now in the Ritual we are told that many Christian parents wish to bless their children, like Jesus, and that, moreover, many popular traditions accord great respect to the blessing given to children by their own parents. It is in these terms that the rite for the blessing of children is conceived. Nevertheless the Ritual also states that if a priest or deacon is present, particularly on the occasion of a visit carried out at set times to bless families, it is for him to exercise this ministry of blessing.

The subject of the ministry of blessing in the Ritual is treated, not in terms of the theology of particular 'powers' and 'effects', but in terms of the theology of the ecclesial manifestation of God's blessing for human beings. The constitution on the liturgy talked about this in its section 79. The Ritual presents it as follows: 'The ministry of blessing is connected with a particular exercise of the priesthood of Christ and according to the place and office which each person holds in the people of God' (*Praenotanda*, 18). By this criterion, we are told that it is appropriate for the bishop to preside over celebrations which affect the whole diocesan community and attract large numbers of people. The priest should celebrate those indicated by the nature of his service to the people of God; he may celebrate all the blessings in the Ritual. The deacon should celebrate those specifically assigned to him. Lay people (specified as 'men and women') have the role of celebrating various blessings related to their own mission (for example, that of children by parents) and, if commissioned, others which cover a wide range, from the blessing of the sick to the blessing of cars and aeroplanes.

On the subject of 'reserved blessings', the Ritual says that the bishop may reserve some blessings to himself if pastoral needs require, blessings which affect the whole diocesan community and are best celebrated with special solemnity. In this way the legal concept of the 'reserved blessing' in fact disappears, being replaced by the pastoral concept of the need for the bishop to be present as the leader of his church.[3]

The definition is therefore broad. There remains some confusion about the commissioning of lay people to preside at certain blessings (which might make sense in the case of blessings affecting the whole community, but seems unnecessary in the case of more private matters), but in general this extension of the authority to preside at blessings seems sufficient to eliminate the image of a hierarchical power capable of obtaining specific benefits. This may, of course, clash with the expectations of some Christian people, who may be surprised to see a lay person—even if commissioned—blessing cars or animals at the traditional ceremonies, but it must be hoped that this surprise will in the end be educative.

3. WHAT IS BLESSED? A QUESTIONABLE CLASSIFICATION

The range of blessings offered by the Ritual is very wide. It is also very varied, going from the sending out of missionaries to grace before meals, via blessings for a religious house, a power station and a cement factory. Clearly, all these moments of ecclesial prayer can be grouped under the title of 'blessing', but the single title may cover rather different meanings in the various cases. The identical structure and content of each blessing in fact demonstrates these different meanings and values. The sending out of missionaries, for example, is given an ecclesial celebration with a definite quasi-sacramental character, and much the same happens with the blessing of a baptistry, where the rite is heavily evocative of baptism. Other blessings, in contrast, have to do with more everyday events and do not seem to fall into the same category; such are the blessing for a mother before childbirth, the blessings for the sick, old people, and so on. Others again, such as the blessings for animals and tools, belong to everyday life, but are less central, and so the series could be continued.

One might have hoped that the arrangement of blessings in the Ritual would indicate these differences of meaning and status. One possible starting point might have been the old distinction between constitutive blessings and invocational blessings. Another would have been the distinction between blessings which fall more within the orbit of sacramental and ecclesial action and those which are intended for the sanctification of situations in ordinary life.[4] A further possibility would have been the classification used by what has been until now the largest collection of blessings, the German benedictional, which distinguishes between blessings belonging to parochial life, blessings belonging to family life, blessings belonging to public life and blessings for general use.[5]

The Ritual, on the other hand, chooses a classification which mixes formal and thematic criteria, by dividing the blessings into the five sections mentioned at the beginning of this article. So in the first section, devoted to blessings for persons, blessings connected with family life (which appear first) and blessings for groups such as a fire brigade are mixed with the quasi-consecratorial blessing of missionaries. The second section, containing blessings for buildings and objects, has the blessing for a new seminary or religious house alongside the blessing of a foundation stone, a factory or a car. The three other sections, in contrast, are more unified: objects and things used or put up in churches, objects of popular devotion, and formulas for general use.

As a result, while the composition of the individual blessings shows an effort to highlight their particular character and meaning (though some formulas are too complicated, and would be better with fewer readings and prayers), when it came to arranging them the editors seem to have lost sight of this criterion. They have therefore produced an equalisation of meanings which perhaps indicates that the important thing here is the power of blessing, which derives from the carrying out of the rite (which applies equally to diverse situations), and not its place in a general theological and ecclesial conception.

4. PERFORMING BLESSINGS OR THE RELATIONSHIP BETWEEN GOD AND THE WORLD

We turn now to the detail of the texts and rites of the blessings. We shall ignore those closely connected with the sacraments (such as those already mentioned, for the sending out of missionaries or for the blessing of a baptistry), since these seem more an extension of directly sacramental theology and liturgy. We noted above that all the blessings take the form of a liturgy of the word, with readings, a prayer of blessing and, in many cases, the possibility of a prayer by the faithful. According to the occasion, there may also be suggestions for psalms, hymns and some sign. The fact that these blessings have this liturgical form is certainly important as a way of emphasising that they are ecclesial gatherings, in which God is listened to, praised and invoked, in contrast to conceptions based on the beneficent powers inherent in particular gestures or prayers. One extension of this which is worth mentioning is the insistence that the blessing of objects or buildings should be carried out in the presence of all those who are in any way affected by what is blessed, since these blessings have their meaning in relation to the people who are going to use the objects or buildings: for example, there is a stipulation that a house should not be blessed except in the presence of the people who are going to live in it.

The matter of signs and rites is also interesting. The general rule is that the prayers should be said with the hands raised or extended, in a gesture indicative of invocation. On the other hand, the ritual of the sign of the cross is not encouraged, no doubt because of the inadequate connotations it may carry. However, another ritual with questionable connotations is encouraged, the sprinkling of water. Even though the Ritual says that when water is sprinkled there should be a reference to its baptismal significance, this ritual in ceremonies of this type carries such strong overtones of purification and sacralisation that it is hardly likely to change its meaning however much explanation is given. Matters are made worse in some cases where forms of aspersion are suggested such as that in the blessing of a foundation stone, where it is suggested that after the stone has been sprinkled the sprinkling should be continued along the boundaries of the space to be occupied by the building. There are also the signs with a closer relation to particular objects, for example the ringing of a bell or the playing of an organ during the blessing of these objects.

The Ritual's intention with respect to signs and rites seems, in short, clear: they should have meaning, but not encourage ideas which are in any way superstitious. In the detail, however, there is sometimes slippage. Despite this the elements of the liturgy of the word contained in the blessings, and the attempt to give meaning and purpose to signs and rites within this liturgy, show this intention to treat the blessings as acts of praise and invocation on the part of the Christian community and signs of the presence of God in the world. The same intention will appear from an analysis of the form taken by the prayers of blessing themselves, of what is prayed for and how it is prayed for.

The prayers of blessing have a very discreet, almost secular, style. This is true, at least, in most cases. What stands out is the praise of God and the asking for his grace. This takes different forms according to the persons or objects being blessed, but is always closely related to the form of any prayer not called a 'blessing'. There is therefore no idea that God is going to grant any particular virtue to the objects being blessed; the prayers are always for those who are to use them or, in the case of buildings, there is a metaphorical request for the presence of God in them for the benefit of those who live in them. There is no suggestion that God should free persons from particular evil presences, nor any claim that the blessing will protect those who receive it from radiation or the economic crisis. The use of the word 'bless' is also discreet, and there seems to be a preference to highlight what is being asked for in the blessing rather than the fact that the rite is a blessing.

5. STRESS ON THE VALUE OF HUMAN ACTIVITY

The introduction to blessings for public services (fire brigades, the Red Cross, etc.) says, 'Faithfully following the Gospel, the Church encourages and supports with its action everything good which is to be found in the human community.' Services of this sort are therefore blessed 'even though they form part of a structure set up by the civil authority'.

The need to justify these blessings in this way is a clear indication that the practice is not clear to everyone. But, however this may be, the fact is that we are given this 'doctrine', that for something to be good it is not necessary for it to be inspired by the Church or engaged in Church activities. In this sense, the texts of the blessings show a tendency to stress the value of the things and activities of this world in themselves. They do so sometimes, indeed, with an exaggerated and almost medieval admiration for 'the wonders of science'. In the majority of cases the texts indicate the value of the things and activities for human progress, give thanks to God for it and pray for human welfare through the object which is being blessed.[6] These prayers also usually indicate the final end of the welfare specified, the praise of God or eternal life. Sometimes a reference to ecclesial action is also added, but in second place. In the blessing of communications media, for example, after saying that they serve mutual assistance between human beings, the promotion of culture and entertainment, the text notes that they can also be used for the propagation of the kingdom of God.

Sometimes, however, the point of view adopted is that things are only of value in so far as they directly assist the faith. For example, in the blessing for a university the petition is that there may flourish in the building attachment to Christ the Teacher and the search for the fount of truth, in a very 'unmodern' attitude to teaching. In the prayer of the faithful, however, the petition is for the progress of human society as a result of research.

Again, the choice of biblical readings is also surprising. Normally they are readings which invite the hearer to recognise the value, in itself, as a created object or a human achievement, of what is being blessed. Nevertheless in particular cases, such as that of means of transport, the criterion changes and allegorical readings are given ('I am the way, the truth and the life'; 'In him we live and move and have our being').[7] This allegorical approach makes sense in relation to activities and objects for religious use (for example, in the blessing for the door of a church), but in the case cited it is rather out of place.

Nevertheless the general tenor is the one described, a stress on created realities and human activity as of worth in themselves, for which we should give thanks and ask God's kindly grace.

6. CHRISTIAN ASPIRATIONS IN THE WORLD: SUCCESS AND PROSPERITY OR JUSTICE, FIDELITY TO THE GOSPEL AND ETERNAL LIFE?

What favours are asked of God in the prayers of blessing? This is an important aspect to consider, since in it we are brought up against the dialectic (or perhaps the contradiction) between natural (religious) aspirations and the suggestions of the Gospel.

In general, the natural aspirations human beings tend to express before God are for liberation from evils and problems, prosperity, and even success in competition with others. On the other hand, the Gospel puts forward a different type of aspiration: justice, service, the welfare of the poor, and an ultimate aspiration, both in terms of religion and of the gospel, eternal life.

The Ritual mixes the two types of aspiration in different degrees (perhaps reflecting the attitudes of different authors). One of the 'natural' aspirations is, however, firmly excluded, the desire for success in competition with other human beings. Part of the same attitude is the explicit rejection of the blessing of weapons. On the other hand, it might be asked whether the uncritical blessing of factories and offices, with no reference to the division and tension between labour and capital, is not a way of blessing the success of some people at the expense of others.[8]

Apart from this aspect, the mixture mentioned above is clear. So in the blessing for a car there is a prayer that no harm may come to the occupants, and at the same time one that the driver may drive safely and help others by his or her prudence. The blessing for children includes a prayer for children who are suffering. The rite for the blessing of a new house, in addition to God's protection and love between husband and wife, asks 'that those who are homeless may receive our help'. In some blessings there is even explicit criticism of an attitude which treats prosperity as the ultimate objective. In the blessing for the fruits of the earth, for example, the prayer asks for prosperity, but also asks that 'in asking God's blessing on the fruit of our labour, we may not forget the fruits of justice we should produce in our lives'. At one point we find a complex blessing which starts from a general attitude of criticism of the system of capitalist organisation. The prayer in this blessing, for a power station, asks that we may use the power of nature for the glory of God and the welfare of human beings, that we may cooperate in renewing the face of the earth, not only with intelligence, but also with justice and charity, that progress may be guided by 'sound minds', that those who are oppressed by unjust discrimination may, with the help of all, come to enjoy the rights and prosperity to which all are entitled.

But attitudes vary from blessing to blessing. There are other blessings in which the object of the prayer is simply protection. In the blessing for a foundation stone, for example, when we might expect petitions similar to those in the blessing of a new house, the prayer simply asks that the building may be successfully completed and that the builders may be protected from harm.

7. THE RITUAL: THE SEARCH FOR A VALID MEANING FOR BLESSINGS

The point of blessings is being questioned, and in many places they are being quietly abandoned. They seem to belong to a bygone religious world, and also to conflict with the secular character of the things of this world, that is, the value they have in themselves, according to the Gospel, without special sacralising processes.

At the same time, however, blessings can also be significant actions, full of the evocative power of faith and human life: signs of the presence of God in all aspects of life, signs of the victory of Jesus Christ over all evil, and signs of faith and of the Christian community. They can be valuable actions provided they are understood in this way and succeed in avoiding any superstitious views of the world or encouraging ideas of the existence of religious powers which can easily obtain specific beneficial effects.[9]

The new Ritual seems to have been compiled, in principle, with this intention, though we have seen places where it is not consistent.

Translated by Francis McDonagh

Notes

1. *Rituale Romanum ex Decreto Sacrosancti Oecumenici Concilii Vaticani II instauratum auctoritate Ioannis Pauli II promulgatum de Benedictionibus* (Rome 1984). (All texts cited are translated from the author's Spanish. *Translator's Note*)

2. Art. 'Benedizione' *Enciclopedia Cattolica* II (Rome 1949) col. 1303.

3. On the other hand the new Code of Canon Law treats the subject as a clearly juridical question (can. 1169). It is not the task of this article to analyse the Code, but it is appropriate at least to note that almost everything the Code says about sacramentals belongs to a mentality which is not that of either the Ritual or the Constitution on the Liturgy. For example, it stresses that sacramentals are instituted and interpreted by the Apostolic See (can. 1167), whereas the *Praenotanda* (33) and the Constitution (37–40, 65) are more open.

4. See *Constitution on the Liturgy*, 60.

5. *Benediktionale. Studienausgabe fur die katholischen Bistümer des deutschen Sprachgebietes* (Freiburg, Vienna, Einsiedeln, Zürich 1979).

6. In this connection it is worth noting also the blessing for a woman before childbirth, which has no hint of any idea that childbirth (and the previous sexual relations) are 'unworthy' and in need of purification. Nevertheless examination of the blessing reveals a subliminal message of depreciation. The text goes on to talk of the dignity of woman as something 'surprising', which women attain thanks to Mary and to the fact that God consented to become a human being in a mother's womb.

7. John 14; Acts 17. In the German benedictional, on the other hand, the reading suggested for the blessing of cars is Tobit 5, the angel who protects the young man's journey, and for the blessing of a plane Sirach 43, the beauty and grandeur of the sky.

8. Here the Ritual seems to be operating with a view of human work which belongs to a previous age. The rubric for the blessing of tools suggests that the rite may be performed solemnly before a gathering of Christian workers invited to attend with their implements of work; is it really envisaged that the owners of the factories and offices concerned will let them bring their lathes and typewriters to be blessed? For a group of self-employed workers with their own equipment such a meeting and blessing could indeed make sense, but this is unlikely to be the situation of the great majority of workers.

9. See J. Aldazabal 'Bendecir tiene todavia sentido' *Phase* 121 (1981) 19–38; M. Löhrer 'Sacramentales' *Sacramentum Mundi* 6 (Barcelona 1976) cols. 157–164.

David Power

Editorial Conclusion: Receiving the Tradition

TO ADDRESS the connection between blessing and power is to take up an issue that is doubly difficult. On the one side, while the Christian tradition of blessings is richly varied, its study risks reducing all blessings to a stereotype. On the other side, power proves to be a concept that is hard to clarify, involving as it does hazy images of divine power and the hazy transactions of power that go on between the givers and the beneficiaries of blessings. Despite these problems, it is the supposition at work in this issue of *Concilium* that whatever else may be addressed in a tradition of blessings, the symbolic reality of divine power that empowers human life and reverses the human condition is a key element in it.

1. IMAGING POWER

A few years ago, the Catholic Theological Society of America at its annual convention addressed the theme of power as an issue in theology .[1] In his presidential address, Leo O'Donovan made the point that while theology has recently had much to say on the exercise of ecclesiastical and social power, it has come to remain somewhat reticent on the theme of God's power.[2] This reticence may be due to the problem of relating a traditional notion of divine omnipotence to the squabblings for power that mark human history, as well as to the apparent powerlessness of the lives of many who are nonetheless dubbed redeemed. It may also have something to do with the seemingly conflicting images of divine power to be found in our traditions, and to the imagery of other powers perpetually in conflict with the divine. It is hard to give clarity to all of this, as well as to the way in which claims to possess the power of the Spirit, or to be able to transmit it, seem to be at odds with one another.

In examining the connection between power and blessing, as this has emerged from the studies presented in this issue or even from the questions that they do not tackle, it is helpful and necessary to distinguish between the more formal liturgical blessings and their euchology on the one hand, and the rather more abundant and untidy world of daily and festive blessings that occur so often on the margins of liturgy on the other. It is true that the canonical tradition of the church, right up to the currently proposed revision of the Roman Ritual, has tried to give discipline and theological nicety to these blessings, but people's practices escape this net to a great extent and image the world of supernatural powers in their own distinctive way. The physical touching of the head with the statue of Saint Roque when his name is invoked is certainly not foreseen in the authorised books, but in some countries if it is omitted the one over whom the prayer is said feels accursed rather than blessed. More commonly, even the most enlightened clergyman finds himself pressured into bestowing blessings on sundry objects of piety on those occasions when he wishes to be totally engaged in the more sublime forms of worship.

2. THE LITURGICAL TRADITION

Some of the discussion about the liturgical tradition of blessing, greatly influenced as it is by studies of *berakah* and *eucharistia*, has currently to do with the appropriate prayer-forms. As I remarked, however, in my own article in this issue, the liturgical canon seems to give witness to a mixture of praise, thanksgiving, petition and exorcism, admitting of no stereotype. It is in the varied interplay of these forms that a community's sense of the divine power in its midst is to a large extent expressed. If tones of praise or thanks have at times prevailed this is likely to have been due to a strong sense of God's presence in its midst and of the recapitulation of all things in Christ. Where petition prevailed, this expressed feelings of powerlessness, either in confronting powers of evil or in dominating the perverse conditions of human living. When powerless in face of nature or of hostile forces, the inclination to look for supernatural intervention is strong, so that requests for blessings *from* God seem to overshadow the blessing *of* God that comes more easily to those who sense the force of creative and redemptive power. It is never possible to interpret past liturgical traditions of blessing without taking account of how a community saw its relation to the world around it, or of the economic and social conditions in which it lived.

The case of the blessing of baptismal waters, which was taken as a paradigm for the study of blessing in this issue of *Concilium*, shows how differently Christian traditions can conceive the world in which the power of Christ works to humanity's redemption. The texts and practices examined in the three articles show that this blessing was never conceived simply as an individual act, as the occasion of doing something to the waters in order to ready them for baptismal immersion. Each liturgy, whether eastern or western, whether medieval or contemporary, images in its blessing a world in which the believing community lives by faith and in which it senses itself empowered by the Spirit and protected against the powers that work for humanity's undoing. The model of the world in which God's power is active is not identical in all the traditions, as Stock and Winkler show, but each liturgy in its own way assimilates the biblical images of empowerment and in its own way associates them with prevailing cultural images of power.

For a people to be effectively empowered for living by blessing, it is necessary that the world imaged be coherent and consistent. Conviction or persuasiveness may be lacking on several counts. There may simply be no coherent vision within which liturgy operates, and that of course is the risk of a time of cultural change, such as we are presently living through. There may also be dissonance between what is expressed and what is lived by the community. Stock remarks on the connection which has to exist between the images of godly and ecclesial fruitfulness invoked in blessing and the actual fruitfulness of the community that blesses the waters. Without a covenant community, the blessing lacks meaning and force. Mpongo's article in particular draws attention to a third source of dissonance, namely, that which may exist between the world of the liturgical text and the broader cultural world within which people live. From his queries about appropriate African celebration, we see how important it is for blessings to take account of indigenous cultural symbols and experiences of power, when invoking God's power. Can liturgy relate the world of redemption to these powers? What have they to do with the body of Christ? Where do they belong in the enduring conflict between the power of God and ungodly powers?

Earlier Christian traditions are not without their own sense of the existence and influence of other powers, as is shown by the joining of exorcism to blessing. One may think that this aspect of life has not always been well handled in Christian ritual, but the practice of blessing cannot ignore how much people feel alienated by subjection to alien powers, or are in fact alienated from their own power by an excessive dependence on supposedly beneficent agents. Redemption promises freedom in the Spirit. Since blessings become part of so many moments of human existence they should offer a way of appropriating this freedom. The insecurity of people's hold on the world has much to do with the excesses in the tradition. Exorcisms proliferate because of fear and because of the inability to find power in the human resources at people's disposal. Everything is blessed because divine protection must be sought at every corner.

One of the deviations in the practice of blessing perhaps less often remarked upon is the inclusion under canonical norms, and within the priestly domain, of many blessings which belong more properly in family life or are more appropriately exchanged among the faithful themselves. The clericalisation of blessings has contributed to a loss of the sense of blessing among the faithful.

The invocation of a blessing by an ordained minister belongs in a community gathering as such, for then the minister presides over the community act of praising God and invoking the Spirit. Acts of blessing outside this context belong no more to the ordained minister than they do to other Christians. The *Apostolic Tradition* of Hippolytus still provides a model for community blessing. Blessings of meal, of food, of oil and of light are done by the bishop when the people are gathered together as a community in Christ. It is very likely that as in the Jewish tradition[3] individuals or households invoked and praised God many times in the course of the day. The community form of blessing is continued today on such occasions as the blessing of a fishing fleet, harvest festivals, the public blessing of transport vehicles, and the like, as well as in churches on the occasion of certain feasts. In as much as these are occasions when the solidarity of community in Christ is expressed and shared, it is fitting to have an ordained minister recite the blessing. It smacks of clericalism to have recourse to a priest for the private blessing of articles put at one's use, whether for piety's sake (scapulars, medals and rosaries) or for utilitarian purposes (cars, ploughs, and the like). This is to attach a quasi-magical power to a priestly blessing, or to simply express a dependency which it is possible to overcome.[4]

3. A PEOPLE'S LANGUAGE

When we look to the wider world of blessings as practised among peoples, including what has just been mentioned, we see more into their own language. Perhaps it is true to say that, together with feasts, it is in the customs of blessing and asking blessing that the religious concepts of a people appear more clearly than anywhere else. Indeed, the historical and still factual connection between blessing and feast is worth noting. The feasts of Mary and the saints have been for centuries important occasions of blessing and exorcism, as has been noted in the important study of A. Franz.[5] Along with this, one has only to think of the blessing of children on patronal feasts, of the fête that surrounds the blessing of the harvest or the fishing fleet, or in more recent times of the connection between high seasons and the *arati* of instruments of labour established in Asian countries under the influence of Hindu traditions.

In fact, in some aspects of this practice one discovers a manipulation of clerical blessings by people caught in situations of weakness and powerlessness, sometimes ecclesiastical and sometimes economic and social. Within the Church, not having much influence over liturgical developments, having a purely passive role in what goes on in celebrations, and not understanding the properly theological sense of worship, the people have often taken a hold of those powers that seemed more accessible to them, either a saint or a priest outside the sanctuary, or both together. People have as it were brought these powers to bear upon their common devotions (rosaries, scapulars, medals, prayer-books) or upon their common needs (in fields, homes, beds, foods, wayward children and wayward husbands).

Unfortunately, this appropriation of the power of blessing can often be in effect an acceptance of a more general powerlessness, a resort to the foreign powers that people find accessible when they find no resource of power in themselves. In this sense, the historical relation of blessing to ecclesiastical and economic powerlessness is all important to note. At the same time, people in using blessings in this way are actually expressing a collective power of which they are not fully conscious and so do not use to its full potential. Indeed, of the language or expression used by people in their resort to the more popular forms of blessing one can repeat what a few years ago A. Aubry wrote in *Concilium* of popular festivity:

> Firstly, it affirms the people's identity, territory, history, roots and economy. Secondly, it points to that people's solidarity with other peasants and stresses the ethnical or class bonds between them, because it is clear that the only real power that the peasantry has is its demographic size and the economic pressure that it can exert as a work-force. Thirdly, it defines the people as being poor and exploited and shows that they are always threatened by the power of the city.[6]

When in fact in the very acts of feast and blessing, people come to a more express sense of this solidarity and identity, they are peculiarly prone to hear the Gospel in a fresh light, if it is addressed to them as God's word to the weak and oppressed, and to come to a consciousness of the gift of the Spirit that constitutes a radical reversal of the human condition. In other words, when the sense of collective identity is joined to the redemptive and liberating memory that is at the heart of Jewish and Christian blessing, the praise of God and the invocation of the Spirit in reference to life's situations of powerlessness can become a liberating force, allowing people to find the ways of being makers of their own history. This would be to continue in our own time that emphasis upon covenant and alliance that Nowell and Fabris have noted in biblical blessing, an emphasis that can come only from a rich memory and a renewal of the memory of liberating event and of the divine compassion shown by Christ upon the cross. Perhaps it is the song of Moses and the song of Mary that provide the best models for a contemporary renewal of a blessing tradition.

Notes

1. The Catholic Theological Society of America *Proceedings of the Thirty-Seventh Annual Convention* (New York 1982).

2. *Ibid.* pp. 67–82.

3. See J. Heinemann *Prayer in the Talmud: Forms and Patterns* (Berlin/New York 1977).

4. In her article in this number of *Concilium*, Walton shows how women are breaking away from this dependency and in their own collective memory finding fresh sources of life and power.

5. Adolph Franz *Die kirchlichen Benediktionen im Mittelalter*, 2 Bd. (Freiburg im Breisgau 1909; facsimile reprint Graz 1960).

6. André Aubry 'The Feast of Peoples and the Explosion of Society—Popular Practice and Liturgical Practice' in *Times of Celebration*, *Concilium* 142 (2/1981) ed. David Power, p. 62. Aubry is of course speaking of a particular situation, that of peasants in Latin America, but in any situation of powerlessness the people's language expresses these three things: their identity, their solidarity, and their distance from those who uphold the established order.

Contributors

FRANÇOISE DOLTO is a medical practitioner, psychiatrist and psychoanalyst, now retired. She practised for more than forty years as a child and adult psychoanalyst in private consultation and in hospitals. Among her most recent works and new editions of earlier books are: *Psychanalyse et pédiatrie* (1971), *Le Cas Dominique* (1971), *Lorsque l'enfant paraît*, 3 vols (1977–1979), *La Difficulté de vivre* (1980), *Au Jeu du désir* (1981). She has also published the following in collaboration with G. Séverin: *L'Evangile au risque de la psychanalyse*, 2 vols (1977–78), *La Foi au risque de la psychanalyse* (1981), *La Sexualité féminine* (1982), *Séminaire de psychanalyse d'enfants* (1983), *L'Image inconsciente du corps* (1984).

RINALDO FABRIS was born in Pavia in Italy in 1936 and took degrees in theology at the University of the Lateran and in biblical studies at the Biblical Institute of Rome. He now teaches New Testament exegesis at the theological school of the seminary of Udine and Gorizia. His published works include a commentary on the gospels of Mark and Luke in *Ivangeli* (1977); a study of the law of liberty in John; commentaries on the letters of the Pauline tradition in *Le lettere di Paolo* (1980); a new translation and commentary on Matthew (1982), and *Gesù di Nazareth*, a history and interpretation (1983).

JOSEP LLIGADAS was born in 1950 in Viladecans (Catalonia, Spain). He is a priest specialising in work with young people. He has a doctorate in theology from the Gregorian University and is at present director of the Centre de Pastoral Litúrgica in Barcelona. In addition to works on the liturgy he has published *Jesús, el Crist* (1973) and *La terra de demá, la terra de Déu* (1984). He is one of the editors of the *Celebrar* series and of the journal *Misa Dominical*.

LAURENT MPONGO, CICM, was born in 1931 at Inongo (Zaire), and was ordained priest in Brussels in 1959. He graduated at the Gregorian University in 1963, and, after specialising in liturgy, received a doctorate in theology from St Anselm's, Rome, in 1966. From 1970 to 1980 he was secretary of the Commission on Evangelism of the Episcopal Conference of Zaire, and shared in the preparation of the new rite for the celebration of the Eucharist, now in experimental use in Zaire. He is at present visiting professor at Maryhill School of Theology in Manila, and at St Anselm's in Rome. Professor Mpongo is the author of a number of articles on Christian liturgy in an African context and of *Pour une anthropologie chrétienne du mariage au Congo* (1968).

IRENE NOWELL, OSB, is a Benedictine of Mount St Scholastica in Atchison, Kansas. She finished her MA in theology at St John's University, Collegeville, Minnesota and received her PhD in biblical studies from the Catholic University of America. She is currently teaching at Benedictine College in Atchison. Her publications include: 'An Exodus Approach to Scripture' *Benedictines* 31 (1976) 81–89, 108–114; 'The Prayer of History' *Sisters Today* 51 (1979) 205–214; 'Turning and Being Turned to the Lord' *Benedictines* 36 (1981–1982) 16–21, 29; 'Food is God's Gift' *Liturgy* 2 (1982) 9–13; 'The Book of Jonah: Repentance and Conversion' *Bible Today* 21 (1983) 363–368; regular contributions to *Homily Service* published by Liturgical Conference; and a forthcoming commentary on the books of Jonah, Tobit and Judith, Collegeville Bible Commentary series, published by the Liturgical Press.

DAVID N. POWER, OMI, was born in Dublin, Ireland, in 1932. A member of the congregation of the Oblates of Mary Immaculate, he was ordained presbyter in 1956. Currently professor of systematic theology and liturgy at the Catholic University of America, Washington, DC, USA. His latest book is *Unsearchable Riches: the Symbolic Nature of Liturgy* (New York 1984).

ALEX STOCK, born at Wellingholzhausen, Germany, in 1937, studied theology at Frankfurt, Innsbruck and Würzburg, and took his degree at Innsbruck. Since 1971 he has been professor of theology and the teaching of theology at Cologne. His publications include: *Umgang mit theologischen Texten* (1974); *Textentfaltungen* (1978); (with M. Wichelhaus) *Ostern in Bildern, Reden, Riten, Geschichten und Gesängen* (1979); (with M. Wichelhaus) *Bildtheologie und Bilddidaktik* (1981).

JEAN-MARIE TILLARD, OP, was born at Saint Pierre et Miquelon in France in 1927. He became a Dominican in 1950. He studied at Rome (philosophy) and at Le Saulchoir in Paris. He was an expert at the Second Vatican Council. Since then, in addition to teaching regularly in the Dominican Faculty in Ottawa, he has been actively engaged with ecumenical questions. He was a member of the Anglican-Roman Catholic Commission ARCIC, vice-president of the Orthodox-Roman Catholic Commission Faith and Order and has written many books and articles on ecumenical subjects, including *L'Eucharistie Pâque de l'Eglise* (1964); *Devant Dieu et pour le monde: le projet des religieux* (1974); *Il y a charisme et charisme* (1977); and *L'Évêque de Rome* (1982). He has written articles for *Irénikon, Lumen Vitae,* the *Nouvelle revue théologique, Proche-Orient Chrétien, One in Christ* and *Midway.*

JANET WALTON, SNJM, was born in 1943 and studied at the Catholic University in Washington, DC, Indiana University, Bloomington, Indiana, and Columbia University, New York, where she completed her doctorate in 1979. Since 1980 she has been coordinator and associate professor of worship at Union Theological Seminary in New York City.

GABRIELE WINKLER studied in Rome, Thessaloniki, Munich and Oxford. She is professor of liturgical science in St John's University, Collegeville, USA. She has written widely on Byzantine, Syrian and Armenian liturgies. Her contributions on Armenian church history (*An Obscure Chapter in Armenian Church History, 428–439*) and on the development of the Armenian Creed (*Armenische Symbolstudien*) are to appear shortly.

BOOKS FROM IGNATIUS PRESS

AVAILABLE THROUGH T & T CLARK

Out of Justice, Peace and Winning the Peace
Edited by James Schall

This important volume contains the complete text of both the Joint Pastoral letters of the West German Bishops and of the French Bishops on war and peace. These letters deserve attention from everyone interested in the issue of nuclear deterrence.

Paperback   *£3.95*

Liberation Theology
James Schall

Drawing on important ecclesiastical documents, as well as contemporary articles from experts in the US and abroad, Fr Schall, an authority on the social issues, gives a thorough and concise treatment of this controversial subject.

Paperback   *£11.95*

The Motherhood of the Church
Henri Cardinal de Lubac

Cardinal de Lubac, one of the foremost contemporary theologians, traces through Christian history and the Scriptures the living tradition of the Church and the paternity of her ministers.

Paperback   *£11.95*

FURTHER IGNATIUS PRESS TITLES ARE ALSO AVAILABLE THROUGH T & T CLARK. FREE CATALOGUE AVAILABLE ON REQUEST.

T & T CLARK LIMITED, 36 GEORGE STREET, EDINBURGH EH2 2LQ, SCOTLAND

MODERN THEOLOGY

Volume 1   No. 2   **Editor: Kenneth Surin**   **January 1985**

CONTENTS

Subscriptions to Volume 1, 1984–5
Published quarterly: October, January, April, July
Individuals: £15.00 (UK) £18.00 (overseas) $25.00 (US) $30.00 (Canada)
Institutions: £30.00 (UK) £35.00 (overseas) $65.00 (US) $72.50 (Canada)

Orders, with remittance, or sample copy requests to: Iris Taylor, Journals Dept., Basil Blackwell, 108 Cowley Road, Oxford OX4 1JF, England.

CONCILIUM

All back issues are still in print: available from bookshops (price £3.75) or direct from the publisher (£3.85/US$7.45/Can$8.55 including postage and packing).

T. & T. CLARK LIMITED
36 George Street, Edinburgh EH2 2LQ, Scotland

CONCILIUM 1983

All back issues are still in print: available from bookshops (price £3.75) or direct from the publisher (£3.85/US$7.45/Can$8.55 including postage and packing).

T. & T. CLARK LTD, 36 GEORGE STREET, EDINBURGH EH2 2LQ, SCOTLAND

CONCILIUM 1984

DIFFERENT THEOLOGIES, COMMON RESPONSIBILITY
Edited by Claude Geffre, Gustavo Gutierrez and Virgil Elizondo

THE ETHICS OF LIBERATION—THE LIBERATION OF ETHICS
Edited by Dietmar Mieth and Jacques Pohier

THE SEXUAL REVOLUTION
Edited by Gregory Baum and John Coleman

THE TRANSMISSION OF FAITH TO THE NEXT GENERATION
Edited by Virgil Elizondo and Norbert Greinacher

THE HOLOCAUST AS INTERRUPTION
Edited by Elisabeth Fiorenza and David Tracy

LA IGLESIA POPULAR: BETWEEN FEAR AND HOPE
Edited by Leonardo Boff and Virgil Elizondo

All back issues are still in print: available from bookshops (price £3.75) or direct from the publisher (£3.85/US$7.45/Can$8.55 including postage and packing).

T. & T. CLARK LTD, 36 GEORGE STREET, EDINBURGH EH2 2LQ, SCOTLAND